THIS BOOK HAS BEEN MADE POSSIBLE BY MANY
PERSONS.

From my late father, The Reverend William
A. Jones, Sr., and my mother, Mary Elizabeth
Jones, I first learned of Jesus Christ and
His desire that all men experience the
abundant life. Dr. Kenneth L. Smith,
my Christian Ethics professor at Crozer
Theological Seminary, sharpened the edges
of my social sensitivity with tools of
faithful Christian scholarship.

For the past sixteen years,
Bethany Baptist Church of Brooklyn,
has given me freedom to think, space
to dream, and patient understanding of
my deep involvement in human affairs.

My family has never permitted
me to be satisfied with present achievement,
and has given continuous encouragement
and assistance in my total ministry and in
the course of this writing. Levone Tobin
of the Bethany church staff read and reread
the manuscript. Patricia Wynn, my secretary,
gave long hours to the arduous task of
typing with a sense of total commitment and
a spirit of Christian love.

Brooklyn, New York
February, 1979

GOD IN THE GHETTO

BY WILLIAM A. JONES, JR.

Progressive Baptist Publishing House
850 North Grove Avenue
Elgin, IL 60120

SPECIAL ACKNOWLEDGEMENT is made to the following for permission to reproduce extracts from copyright materials:

New York: Charles Scribner's Sons: *Racism and the Christian Understanding of Man,* by George D. Kelsey, © 1965; *The Social Teachings of the Prophets and Jesus,* by Charles Foster Kent, © 1917; *The Children of Light and Darkness,* by Reinhold Niebuhr, © 1944.

New York: Harper & Row Publishers, Inc.: *Biblical Faith and Social Ethics,* by Clinton Gardner, © 1960; *Dark Ghetto,* by Kenneth E. Clark, © 1965; *The Nixon Theology,* by Charles P. Henderson, Jr., © 1972; *The Racial Problem in Christian Perspective,* by Kyle Haseldon, © 1959; *Morality and Beyond,* by Paul Tillich, © 1954.

New York: Seabury Press: *Black Theology and Black Power,* by James H. Cone, © 1969; *Violence,* by Jacques Ellul, © 1969.

New York: Fawcett World Library: *The Souls of Black Folk,* by W. E. Burghardt DuBois, © 1961.

New York: Monthly Review Press: *The Pillage of the Third World,* by Pierre Jalee, Copyright © 1968 by Monthly Review Press. First published in France, Copyright © 1965 by Francois Maspero. Reprinted by permission of Monthly Review Press.

Nashville, Tenn.:   Abingdon Press: *Unyoung-Uncolored-Unpoor,* by Colin Morris, © 1969.

Philadelphia, Pa.:   University of Pennsylvania: *The Philadelphia Negro,* by W. E. Burghardt DuBois, © 1899.

New York: Random House, Inc.: *Points of Rebellion,* by William O. Douglas, © 1970.

New York: G. P. Putnam's Sons: *The Issue of Black Survival in America,* by Samuel F. Yette, © 1971.

Cover photo by Cheryl Fort

GOD IN THE GHETTO

Progressive Baptist Publishing House, Elgin, IL 60120

Printed in the United States of America
Library of Congress Catalog Number: 78-71193
ISBN: 0-89191-134-0

5

Geneva, Switzerland, for permission to quote from *Theology of Culture,* by Paul Tillich, © 1959. Originally published in *World Christian Education,* 2nd Quarter, 1966.

Washington, D.C.: Associated Publisher, Inc.: *Richard Allen, An Apostle of Freedom,* by Charles H. Wesley, © 1935.

ADDITIONAL ACKNOWLEDGEMENTS

Lester Bristown and Paul Cornley. Paper read before Senate Committee on Nutrition and Human Needs, Washington, D.C., November 3, 1969.

H. Joseph Fichter, American Religion and the Negro, Daedalus, 94, No. 4 Richmond © 1965, Harold R. Isaacs, Group Identity and Political Change: The Role of Color and Physical Characteristics, Daedalus, 96, No. 2, © 1967. Used by permission.

Detroit Industrial Mission, Racism Isn't Just, Life and Work, 11, No. 2, © 1971.

The Boston Globe, December 21, 1971; *The Boston Sunday Herald,* October 2, 1966.

The Works of Aristotle, Vol. II. *The Great Books of the Western World,* edited by Robert H. Hutchins, Chicago, *Encyclopedia Britannica,* 1952.

The Boston Black People's Situation and the Challenge to the Boston Black Community, manuscript, by Virgil Woods, 1972.

The American Democrat: On Hints on the Social and Civic Relations of the United States of America, by James F. Cooper, © 1838, Phinney, Cooperstown, N.Y.

CONTENTS

Page

Preface

Part I
GOD IN THE GHETTO

Part II
SERMONS

DEDICATED
to my Children

Part I

GOD
IN THE
GHETTO

1

The System

IN AMERICAN SOCIETY A NUMBER OF "UMBRELLA" TERMS HAVE DEVELOPED which represent symbolically those collective forces that serve to deny, demean, and dehumanize large, nonaffluent segments of the population. Terms such as *the white power structure, the man, the devil, Pharaoh, Uncle Bubba,* and *the system* are key words in ghetto rhetoric. Their usage extends even to more affluent members of the larger white society, who are disenchanted and disaffected by the existing arrangement in the nation. To regard these umbrella terms as simple slang, uttered mainly by uninformed, shiftless youths, is to miss their meaning, for they encompass a body of beliefs and an in-depth analysis as sweeping and as penetrating as the nation's ills. They cover "a multitude of sins." In fact, they are the verbal symbols of the old, deep, unabated groanings of the oppressed. When the alienated and afflicted speak of "The System," the connotations are clear; they have engaged in serious scrutiny as a result of their own pain predicament, and have concluded that their victimization is neither an accident of creation nor of history, but rather the result of a skillfully designed pattern of systematic exclusion from the mainstream of American culture.

"The System" refers implicitly to the American trinity of capitalism, racism, and militarism. Capitalism is the economic system. Erected on the damnable foundation of slave labor, it pyramided on cheap labor after the emancipation and now thrives on social stratification, which is racism made manifest. Racism serves to preserve and perpetuate the system. Militarism, the formula's third ingredient, has almost become a political necessity. It is not mere happenstance that the nation has known no real peace for more than three decades. Militarism saps the mental and physical energies of the nation's youth, those most capable of creatively confronting the evils of racism and capitalism.

A gravestone in a cemetery in Japan bears the inscription:

> Here lies a Black man
> Who fought the Yellow man
> For what the White man
> Took from the Red man.

This inscription depicts simply and succinctly the American trinity of capitalism, racism, and militarism. Frederick Douglass, in his celebrated Fourth of July speech, declared that "for revolting barbarity and shameless hypocrisy, America reigns without a rival. . . . America is false to the past, false to the present, and solemnly binds herself to be false to the future."[1] The prevailing barbarity and continuing falsity produce the swelling chorus of dismay and discontent.

Historically, the nation has been long on promise and short on performance. The American promise contained in the Declaration of Independence is probably the most humane ever reduced to language. "We hold these Truths to be self-evident, that all Men are created equal, that they are endowed by their Creator with certain unalienable Rights, that among these are Life, Liberty, and the Pursuit of Happiness."[2] The promise embedded in these words is theologically correct and anthropologically sound. The democratic ethic, representing the ideal with respect to the historic social experiment, is rooted in religious realism and grounded in the Christian doctrine of man. Reinhold Niebuhr's famous epigram puts it well: "Man's capacity for justice makes democracy possible, but man's inclination to injustice makes democracy necessary."[3]

Man has the capacity for justice and injustice, for creativity and destructivity. In America necessity has perenially outweighed capacity. The democratic ideal has yet to flower. Irrespective of constitutional guarantees, congressional acts, presidential pronouncements, and denominational proclamations, America must be viewed through the lenses of microscopic realism rather than those of telescopic idealism. This was to be that place under the sun where freedom's flag waved in the interest of all, but!—How bright with promise was the nation's beginning, but!—What a glorious harvest her springtime promised, but!—Every attempt to articulate the nation's glory serves only to dramatize her shame. A simple, surface diagnosis of "The System" reveals a sick sociology based on a faulty anthropology, which emanates from a false theology. A man's attitude toward other men reflects the nature of his ultimate values.

When sin becomes structured and inequity institutionalized, the resulant arrangement is ineluctably wicked and nefarious, for it denies others access to "the tree of life." This is the continuing tragedy of America. Victims are correct when they speak of the nation in terms of "The System," for they correctly address that power arrangement in society based on wealth and whiteness which prevents the gap from closing between the needy and the greedy. "The System" is racist to the core. So deep and pervasive in the reality that its bitter fruits multiply even without cultivation.

To label a society racist is to make a rather sweeping judgment. It is to assert unequivocally that there is at work within the body politic a master-race ethos, which has been described as "the eternal joke played on conscious culture at the expense of unconscious biology." What is racism? *Webster's Third New World Dictionary* defines it as: (1) "the assumption that psychocultural traits and capacities are determined by biological race and that races differ decisively from one another which is usually coupled with a belief in the inherent superiority of a particular race and its right to domination over others," and (2) "a doctrine or political program based on the assumption of racism and designed to execute its principles." Each aspect of the preceding definition is part and parcel of the American scenario—the doctrinal and the programmatic aspects.

To be sure, racism's programmatic expressions are not as overt as they once were. The apartheid of the pre-1863 era is virtually nonexistent. The dehumanizing features and symbols of the period of racial segregation, such as separate rest rooms and water fountains, segregated transportation, and the Niggers Not Allowed signs, are no longer present. However, the absence of overt expressions does not spell the demise of covert realities. Will D. Campbell and James J. Holloway state succinctly that nothing has changed. We have the milestones—the 1954 court decision and the '55, '56, '57, '58, and '59 supporting decisions outlawing one racist gimmick after another. We have Mrs. Rosa Parks, who because her feet hurt, would not move to the back of the bus, and we have the Montgomery Improvement Association which that act set off. We have the milestone of 1960—the sit in movement and the organization of SNCC. We have the Washington March, the Civil Rights Act of 1964 and the Civil Rights Acts of 1965, etc. But despite the milestones, nothing has changed in the relationships between Black people and White people.[4]

If relationships are determinative in evaluating the social or human posture of people, the racist label appropriately applies to America. For relationships not only have to do with psycho-social attitudes, but with sharing resources and distributing power.

What are the marks of a racist society? Robert W. Terry cites four essential marks: "power disproportionately distributed, denial of access to resources and institutions, ethnocentric (superior) standards, and misplacement of the problem, all of which are based on color differences."[5] Reporting on the results of an experiment titled "White Racism by Design," Terry writes:

By being a normal, everyday citizen, by doing business as usual, racism flourished. To be anti-racist meant confronting the basic arrangements and norms of American life. Although a painful learning, the group realized that to be anti-racist was subversive of the presently practiced American dream.[6]

The logical conclusion is apparent: To be antiracist is to be anti-American.

American racism is predicated on color differences. Harold R. Isaacs sums up the determinative influence of color:

> Skin color has served as the badge of master and subject, of the enslaved and the free, the dominators and the dominated. Of all the factors involved in the great rearrangement of human relationships taking place today, skin color is the most glandular.[7]

Color is a condition that blacks cannot alter, one that they do not desire to alter. Because of the badge of blackness, they belong to the largest permanent minority in America. Annihilation of the race problem by amalgamation is not on the black agenda. Racism is regarded by blacks as white sickness and is, therefore, a white problem. No conscientious national effort has been made to remove the racist cancer.

Twenty-five years before the end of slavery, James Fennimore Cooper warned his countrymen:

> The time must come when American slavery shall cease and when that day shall arrive (unless early and effectual means are devised to obviate it) two races will exist in the same region, whose feelings will be embittered by inextinguishable hatred, and who carry on their faces the respective stamp of their factions. The struggle that will follow will necessarily be a war of extermination. The evil day may be delayed, but can scarcely be averted.[8]

More than a century after emancipation, the National Advisory Commission on Civil Disorders stated:

> The nation is rapidly moving toward two increasingly separate Americas . . . a white society principally located in suburbs, in smaller central cities, and in the peripheral parts of large central cities; and a Negro society largely concentrated within large central cities.[9]

The commission concluded that "white racism is essentially responsible for the explosive mixture which has been accumulating in our cities since the end of World War II."[10]

The two Americas of which the Kerner Commission speaks are in fact already existing. Polarization is no developing phenomenon; it is as ancient as the slave system. And in spite of the deathblow that has been dealt to legal segregation, the basic institutions of American society remain sharply segregated. Blacks and whites do not work or play on a peer basis. Skin color remains the basis for white decisions affecting the lives of all citizens. White superordination and black subordination is the norm in white-black relations as far as the white majority is concerned. The hard, brutal realities of the racist ethos touch and affect the lives of all black people. This ethos is the root cause of their common affliction, and nowhere is the reality more poignant and pointed than in the phenomenon called the ghetto.

FOOTNOTES

1. Frederick Douglass in an address entitled "The American Fourth of July Celebration" at Rochester, N.Y., July 4, 1852.

2. The Declaration of Independence.

3. Reinhold Niebuhr, *The Children of Light and the Children of Darkness*, p. xi.

4. Will D. Campbell and James J. Holloway, *Up to Our Steeples in Politics*, pp. 53-54.

5. Robert W. Terry, "Racism Isn't Just . . .," *Life & Work* 13, no. 2 (Summer 1971): 1.

6. Ibid.

7. Harold R. Isaacs, "Group Identity and Political Change: The Role of Color and Physical Characteristics," *Daedalus* 96 (1967): p. 353.

8. James Fennimore Cooper, *The American Democrat: On Hints on the Social and Civic Relations of the United States of America,* p. 167.

9. *Report of the National Advisory Commission on Civil Disorders,* Otto Kerner, chairman, p. 407.

10. Ibid., p. 203.

2

The Ghetto:
Symbol of the System

THE WORD *ghetto* FIRST CAME INTO USAGE in Venice during the sixteenth century, when it was applied to the section where the Jewish colony lived. Its etymology is traced to the Latin *jactare*, meaning to throw, cast, or discard. The Kerner Commission defined a ghetto as "any area within a city characterized by poverty and acute social disorganization, and inhabited by members of a racial or ethnic group under conditions of involuntary segregation."[1] In America the designation is almost completely synonymous with the black community. *Ghetto* connotes racial, social, and economic oppression. Kenneth Clark in his definitive study *Dark Ghetto* gives a clear portrait of the phenomenon:

> The dark ghetto's invisible walls have been erected by the white society, by those who have power, both to confine

19

those who have no power and to perpetuate their power-lessness. The dark ghettos are social, political, educational, and—above all—economic colonies. Their inhabitants are subject peoples, victims of the greed, cruelty, insensitivity, guilt, and fear of their masters.[2]

Communities such as Harlem, Bedford-Stuyvesant, Watts, and Chicago's Southside have long been the sociologist's bailiwicks for ghetto studies. So deep is the pain and so pervasive the squalor that Clark's use of the adjective *dark* is not accidental. In America, *dark, ugly,* and *black* are almost interchangeable. Because of the implications of utter misery, helplessness, and hopelessness, certain blacks have a deep abhorrence of the word *ghetto.* Use of the word on public platforms nearly always elicits a refutation by some blacks who feel that their self-esteem has been assaulted. On the basis of such pride, there is an intense desire to move out of the ghetto to escape the physical and psychological havoc usually ascribed to life there. However, for blacks there is "no hiding place." Assimilation is impossible, for acceptance by whites is at best nominal and superficial. No amount of social acculturation will dissipate the badge of blackness; it is an enduring reality. Hence, the ghetto is not purely geographic. It reaches past slum tenements, dirty streets, absentee landlords, and crowded apartments; it goes beyond certain neighborhood boundaries; it extends to a definite cultural condition. At rock-bottom the ghetto is a non-geographic entity, a social perimeter of pain determined by pigmentation.

The Kerner Commission made a fundamental error by attempting to localize the ghetto as a certain "area within a city." Clark, on the other hand, clearly understood the boundless dimensions of the reality:

Though many middle-class residents of the ghetto do

have a constant wish for physical and psychological escape, the ghetto has a devouring quality and to leave
provokes a curious struggle. In an important sense no
one can ever leave.[3]

Although acute suffering and deprivation are localized
enough to call certain sections "ghettos," the ghetto is
essentially as boundless as blackness.

The ghetto is the most profound and visible symbol of
the system. Without its existence, there would be no need
for the derisive terms employed to characterize America.
In substance, a symbol is an idea objectified. The ghetto is
an idea clearly objectified; it is a clear manifestation of
how white America views and regards blacks in America.
Created by whites, it is condoned and maintained by
them.

The rise and development of the ghetto are easy to
trace. Given the white master-race complex which permitted human slavery in America, the development of
the ghetto phenomenon was practically inevitable. The
Emancipation Proclamation did not have the power to
lift blacks from subhuman to human status in the white
psyche. The abolition of slavery as a legally sanctioned
institution could not possibly alter the fractional designation from "three-fifths of a man" to five-fifths.

President Abraham Lincoln's issuance of the Emancipation Proclamation was predicated on political concerns
more than on humane considerations, for his concept of
freedom for blacks did not include social and political
equality. Although he is personally credited with freeing
the slaves, in a real sense he fired them. The promise of
"forty acres and a mule" was never fulfilled. Instead,
ex-slaves were subjected to a new existence for which
they were ill-prepared, because they were handed the
audacious responsibility of lifting themselves by their

21

own bootstraps. Political gains realized in the Reconstruction era were short-lived, for racism was too deeply engrained in the nation's conscience. Social segregation and economic discrimination forced blacks into solidarity for survival's sake. Lynchings were commonplace, the Ku Klux Klan rode with almost total license, and states' rights were sacrosanct. The nation was without a moral conscience. Most blacks had little to look forward to except a life of toil and sweat beneath the burning sun in the fields of Dixie. In 1910, 75 percent of all blacks lived in the rural South, shackled and bruised by the iron chains of segregation. Before the mass migrations, large numbers of blacks sought deliverance through relocation:

> Pinned against the wall by lynchings, proscription, and organized programs, with every man's hand raised against them, Negroes flopped about aimlessly, like fish caught in a net. Intolerably oppressed by conditions which they did not understand and which they could not control, they moved from here to there and back again, from one state to another, from one country to another, from the hills to the delta, from one miserable hut to another ten miles down the road. In the "Exodus of 1879," some 40,000 Negroes stampeded out of the South to the Midwest. Random movements continued throughout the period. A group left Alabama and went to Mexico and starved and came back again. Some went to Canada. Some went to Africa.[4]

These erratic wanderings typified the deep thirst and the insatiable appetite for full freedom impossible to realize in the cruel and callous South. They were the antecedents of the great migration which began in 1915. The North was seen as the promised land, a type of Canaan, flowing with milk and honey. Lerone Bennett describes the pilgrimage in picturesque and yet pathetic language:

With cardboard boxes and brown bags smeared with the grease of fried chickens, with thin clothes pitifully inadequate for Northern winters, hundreds of thousands of Negroes hit the road. They came from the docks of Norfolk and Mobile, from the cotton fields of Mississippi, from kitchens and washtubs, from a thousand crossroads and hamlets, from Waycross, Georgia, and Shubuta, Mississippi, from Memphis, and Jackson and New Orleans, and Little Rock. Almost two million of them came in the greatest internal migration in modern history.[5]

They were not immigrants from a far country. Racism made them "gerim," resident aliens, strangers, and pilgrims in the land of their birth. Through the '20s, the '30s, and the '40s the migration continued, and by 1970, 70 percent of all blacks were located in large metropolitan areas. Breathing space under the visible heel of white tyranny was replaced by crowded conditions beneath an insidious tyranny that in some ways was more devasting. So intent and complete is the ghettoization process, it is estimated that in order to create an unsegregated population housing-wise, 86 percent of all blacks would have to move. But even if this occurred (and there is no reason to suppose that it will), it would not abolish the ghetto, for the ghetto is fundamentally psychocultural and not geographic. Racism is the creator and preserver of the ghetto phenomenon. The consequences are both disastrous and damnable. W. E. Burghardt DuBois's eulogy to his deceased son, "Of the Passing of the First Born," written more than seventy years ago, bespeaks a sweet sorrow that can be shared even now by racism's victims:

All that day and all that night there sat an awful gladness in my heart,—nay, blame me not if I see the world thus darkly through the veil,—and my soul whispers ever to me, saying, "Not dead, not dead, but escaped; not bond, but free." No bitter meanness now shall sicken his baby heart till it die a living death, no taunt shall madden his happy boyhood. Fool that I was to think or wish that this little soul should grow choked and deformed within the Veil! I might have known that yonder deep unworldly look that ever and anon floated past his eyes was peering far beyond this narrow Now. In the poise of his little curl-crowned head did not there sit all that wild pride of being which his father had hardly crushed in his own heart? For what, forsooth, shall a Negro want with pride amid the studied humiliations of fifty-million fellows? Well sped, my boy, before the world had dubbed your ambitions insolence, had held your ideals unattainable and taught you to cringe and bow. Better for this nameless void that stops my life than a sea of sorrow for you. Idle words; he might have borne his burden more bravely than we,—aye, and found it lighter too, some day; for surely, surely this is not the end. Surely there shall yet dawn some mighty morning to lift the Veil and set the prisoned free. Not for me,—I shall die in my bonds,—but for fresh young souls who have not known the night and waken to the morning; a morning when men ask of the workman, not "Is he white?" but "Can he work?" When men ask artists, not "Are they black?" but "Do they know?"[6]

The essence of DuBois's elegy is echoed daily wherever blackness is found in the land.

If the ghetto is truly symbolic of "The System," the objectification of white superiority is seen most clearly in the economics of racism. "The dark ghetto is not a viable community. It cannot support its people; most have to leave it for their daily jobs. Its businesses are geared toward the satisfaction of personal needs and are marginal to the economy of the city as a whole."[7] The statistics present a deplorable picture, though they cannot be considered valid, for ghetto dwellers have never been fully counted by the Bureau of the Census. According to the official statistics, the black unemployment rate is twice that of the white rate. Over 40 percent of all black youths are unemployed. The black underemployment rate is around 40 percent, which means that 40 percent of all blacks who work do so at a level beneath their capacity. The median income gap between black and white families is $7,498 per annum. The result is an island of poverty in the midst of a sea of affluence, and the attending ills are legion.

Blacks are a colonized people. The period of chattel slavery was marked by capitalistic ownership, with each slave master the complete owner of his slaves. Blacks are now victims of socialistic ownership; they are owned by "The System." For what is a ghetto other than a plantation without physical fences? Each workday morning the natives leave the island, the colony, or the reservation and travel to the mainland, where they expend their best energies in the continuing enhancement of the larger, dominant society. Then at eventide they return to the island, tired and worn, and devoid of the energies needed to deal creatively with their own destitution.

Moreover, the situation grows worse because the base of the economic pyramid is broadening, not arithmetically but geometrically. The masses, both black and white, are victimized by the classes. But because of the racist ethos, suffering whites have little desire to make common cause with their black brothers in tribulation. They, along with many blacks, hug an illusion with respect to the so-called ladder of success, a mythological ladder that blinds already weakened eyes to the reality of an upside-down welfare state with socialism for the rich and capitalism for the poor. The rich are on welfare but under other names, such as tax breaks, farm subsidies, airline subsidies, oil depletion allowances, and business bailouts, for example, Lockheed Aircraft Corporation. William O. Douglas correctly states concerning the powers-that-be:

> They accept that degree of socialism implicit in the vast
> subsidies to the military-industrial complex, but not that
> type of socialism which maintains public projects for the
> disemployed and the unemployed alike.[8]

Colin Morris is even more pointed:

> Governments don't feel shame, and it is government by
> the rich for the rich that guards the gap between the
> Haves and the Havenots against shrinkage during our
> lifetime or anyone else's short of bloody revolution.[9]

Persons consigned to gruesome ghettos are given a
steady dose of rhetoric on how their deliverance can be
effected. One cure-all repeatedly offered is that of taking
full advantage of the educational process. But public
education has always been the servant of the very system
that excludes and dehumanizes. Miseducation is the rule
rather than the exception in the ghetto. Public schools in
Bedford-Stuyvesant, for example, are plagued by drop-
outs, flunk outs, and push outs, but this is not due to a
lack of native ability. One cardinal problem is the preponderance of white teachers who have no basic affinity
with the students. Teachers in New York City are pre-
dominantly white, while the pupils are overwhelmingly
black and Puerto Rican. Black children are not innately
inferior. In the main, they are the offspring of parents
who themselves suffered the consequences of inadequate
education and miseducation, and they bear the burden
of the absence of black teachers who once sat where they
now sit. The impact of the educational process failures is
felt most severely when entrance is sought to the
employment arena, where they meet new and novel
categories unrelated to their training and experience.
Government, business, labor, and education work in col-
lusion to produce this typical situation:

Let's give them a test. Those who make the highest score will get the job. Guess who gets the job? The tests are written by people who for the most part know about pheasant-under-glass. If you ask some ghetto child about pheasant-under-glass, he makes zero. But ask him about the breeding habits of cockroaches or how a rat can crawl up an iron crib and gnaw the toes and fingers of his baby sister, and he will make a good grade while the middle-class applicant will make zero. Thus we have the modern idol of merit employment.[10]

It is little wonder that defeatism is so pronounced in the captive community.

In the Nixon era, a new economic preachment came forward called black capitalism. At best, it is too little, too late. The gap is too great to be bridged. The disparity between leading black businesses and major white businesses is worse than shocking. For example, the nation's largest black bank ranks number 1,542 in size, and the nation's largest black insurance company is 1/300th the size of Prudential Life. Black capitalism is pure myth. Arnold Schuchter's comments dispel the myth and make plain the reality:

Whereas white America in large numbers is crossing the threshold of post-industrial society, blacks have not even fully entered the industrial age. "Black Capitalism" has stressed the need for black entrepreneurial opportunities in the internal combustion civilization, while the infra-stucture of electronics, cybernation, communication, and data processing civilization is moving toward dominance over machine and process technology.[11]

Racism's economic consequences are devastating. The black man's economic wings have been cut, so he is unable to fly in the existing capitalistic system. A man's earning power determines how his family lives, the schools his children attend, the clothes they wear, and the food they eat. After 116 years of slavery, blacks have access without assets, and freedom without finance, which is tantamount to existence without equity. In light of the widening economic gap and the broadening base of the economic pyramid, Michael Harrington's prophecy of doom is probably valid:

> The key to the dark vision is this: that trade-unionists, Negroes and the poor will struggle against one another for scarce resources such as housing, jobs and adequate education. Their strife will make even traditional, liberal reform impossible, a fact that will guarantee that there will be even less to go around and therefore more reason to fight. The poor, both black and white, will suffer most egregiously, but the organized workers will have to become paranoid in order to hold onto their possessions. The social fabric of the nation will, of course, be torn to shreds.[12]

The ghetto, symbol of the system, created and preserved by racism, is antithetical to the nation's peace, its well-being, and possibly its continuing existence.

The ghetto in America does not exist in isolation. It is experientially related to people of color in other parts of the world who are inhabitants of the larger ghetto.

FOOTNOTES

1. *Report of the National Advisory Commission on Civil Disorders,* Otto Kerner, Chairman, p. 12. (I criticize this definition elsewhere.)

2. Kenneth B. Clark, *Dark Ghetto,* p. 11.

3. Clark, p. 62.

4. Lerone Bennett, Jr., *Before the Mayflower: A History of the Negro in America,* p. 236.

5. Ibid., pp. 288-89.

6. W. E. Burghardt DuBois, *The Souls of Black Folk,* pp. 155-56.

7. Clark, p. 27.

8. William O. Douglas, *Points of Rebellion,* p. 68.

9. Colin Morris, *Unyoung–Uncolored–Unpoor,* p. 66.

10. Will D. Campbell and James J. Holloway, *Up to Our Steeples in Politics,* p. 132.

11. Arnold Schuchter, *Reparations,* pp. 281-82.

12. Michael Harrington, *Toward a Democratic Left,* pp. 281-82.

3

The Larger Ghetto

REGARDLESS OF LOCALE and whether or not the people are Black American, Caribbean, Latin American, Asian, or African, they are all drawn together by a common affliction into the larger ghetto. Their hopes and aims are essentially one: to challenge a common enemy and rid themselves of the yoke of human tyranny.

In 1900 at the first Pan-African Congress in London, W. E. B. DuBois stated in prophetic terms:

> The problem of the twentieth century is the problem of the color-line,—the relation of the darker to the lighter races of men in Asia and Africa, in America and the islands of the sea.[1]

DuBois lived to see the painful fulfillment of his prophecy and the division of the earth into three distinguishable segments: the capitalist nations, the socialist states, and the third world. The latter constitutes the larger ghetto. Pierre Jalee, a French economist, makes this breakdown of the earth's peoples:

1. **Socialist Group:**
   Soviet Union, European People's Democracies (including Yugoslavia), China, Mongolia, North Korea, North Vietnam, Cuba.

2. **Capitalist Group:**
   (a) Imperialist Zone: United States and Canada, Europe (excluding the Soviet Union and the People's Democracies), Japan, Israel, Australia, and New Zealand.

   (b) Third World: Latin America (excluding Cuba); the whole of Africa; Asia (excluding its socialist countries, Japan and Israel); Oceania (excluding Australia and New Zealand).[2]

Jalee admits that his political and economic division of some countries is open to question. His placement of the third world in the capitalist group does precipitate a real problem. Admittedly, the economies of these states are essentially capitalist, but are they capitalist by choice or by constraint? In most, if not all instances, these countries were forced into the capitalist camp by the military exploits of colonial powers. It is generally agreed, for example, that private ownership, the chief cornerstone of capitalism, was totally foreign to the African ethos and remains alien in large measure to the African spirit.

Jalee is eminently correct when he says that "the so-called Third World is no more than the backyard of imperialism."[3] The third world is inseparably related to the capitalist nations, but not on any equitable basis; the relationship is closer to that of slave and master. There is a negative correlation between population and power, between land area and affluence. Third world peoples constitute nearly half the world's population and occupy over half the world's land area, but in the realm of power—production and trade—they are at the bottom of the world economic ladder. Drawing upon United Nations statistics, Jalee points out the tremendous imbalance of power. In terms of production, capitalist nations control 73.4 percent of the extractive industries and 92.7 percent of the manufacturing industries, while the percentages for third world countries are 26.6 percent and 7.3 percent for the respective industries. With regard to trade, exchange is grossly inequitable. The third world exports natural resources and raw products, and then imports finished goods and products at inordinate prices. Imperialist countries trade mainly with one another (73.5 percent of their total trade). Socialist countries behave in like manner (65 percent of their total trade). But third world countries rarely trade with one another (only 20 percent). Seventy-four percent of their trade is with imperialist countries, due primarily to the dependent status of third world countries, a dependence created and cultivated by and through long years of colonial rule.[4]

In the area of capital relations, the attitude of capitalist countries is at best one of paternalistic arrogance. Foreign aid in loans and grants is administered and allocated mainly on the basis of self-interest. Nations of less strategic importance receive less than others. Imperialism, therefore, is a political-economic phenomenon "implying certain relationships in the international division of labor, in trade and the movement of capital."[5] So interwoven are political considerations and economic interests that moral and humane values are almost impossible to detect. Jean Lacouture's comments are clearly on target:

> The best definition of neo-colonialism is perhaps as a situation in which rich countries invest in poor ones more for the benefit of the giver than of the recipient, and within the latter more for the benefit of the ruling groups than for that of the masses.[6]

The result of this situation is political servitude and economic subjection. High above the stark realities of poverty and hunger in the third world, a battle takes place which upon close examination is purely mythological. Popular thought views the great struggle in the world as one of ideological conflict between democracy and communism or between capitalism and socialism. The underdeveloped countries are caught in the middle and expected to choose between the two warring powers. However, the actual battle is between imperialism and the third world, between the haves and the have-nots. International cartels, supported by cooperating governments, have a noose tightly drawn about the necks of poor people in Asia, Africa, Latin America, the Caribbean, and the United States of America. Huge American corporations reap astronomical profits as a result of foreign-based installations that pay pitifully low wages to native personnel. Decolonization has occurred only in the political area. Those nations in Africa and the Caribbean which have been granted independence from colonial rule are still under the economic rule of the former colonial powers. Economic colonization remains a poignant reality.

What is the chief criterion for membership in the third world? Political ideology? Social philosophy? Economic stance? No, it is none of these. A casual, airplane view of the third world landscape reveals that the masses of the

33

poor, uneducated, and exploited are black, brown, and yellow—the nonwhite peoples. Color is the chief criterion in defining that almost numberless mass called the third world. Though separated by oceans, languages, and cultural differences, they are bound together by three significant factors: (1) their nonwhiteness; (2) a common affliction imposed by a common enemy; and (3) their determination to be free. Jamaican Senator Dudley Thompson, in addressing Black Expo in New York City on October 7, 1972, declared, "The blood that unites us is thicker than the water that divides us." Citizenship in the larger ghetto (the third world) is based almost exclusively on color.

The larger ghetto is dominated and controlled by a ruling triumvirate that Colin Morris euphonically describes as "Unyoung, Uncolored, Unpoor."[7] Their power is tremendously disproportionate to their numbers and it is awesome. They control the means of production and manipulate world politics.

> As the Prayer Book never said, they are all the same sort and condition of men—white, well-nourished, and vastly experienced. To protect their interests, wars are engineered, dictators made and broken, governments bought and sold, currencies adjusted, and markets rigged. They preside over a vast Aladdin's cave into which a ragged world brings its treasure and where fewer and fewer get more and more. They are unbeatable because they make the rules. Even your cry of outrage is rendered meaningless because they own the very language you use. As they leave your mouth, your words are twisted and remolded so that your abuse rings out like a hallelujah to their benevolence. Freedom is what they mean by freedom, democracy is what they mean by democracy, and they have the power to make their definitions stick.[8]

The scenario is replete with dismay and despair. Is

there hope for the inhabitants of the larger ghetto? Can they possibly overcome long-standing injustices that have rendered them powerless in a world where almost absolute power is vested in the hands of a privileged few?

Four hopeful signs appear:

1. Protestation by youth around the world. Young people throughout the world are developing a profound distaste for synthetic values, degenerate democracy, fallacious freedom, and adult hypocrisy.

2. The movements of Pan-Africanism and Negritude. Implicit in both of these is a deep racial consciousness which serves as the motivating force for political and economic self-determination.

3. The dependence of imperialists on the third world for vital energy resources. The underdeveloped nations are rich in raw materials essential to heavy industries. The world energy crisis which steadily worsens is a clear indication that for the first time in modern history, third world people have the upper hand in a matter essential to human existence.

4. Imperialists are the least prepared people for the continuing conflict and struggle. Third world people are on the bottom. Consequently, their pain quotient is significantly higher. They have practically nothing to lose. They are free not only to live, but free to die in the pursuit of justice.

The ruling triumvirate is obviously oblivious to one historical reality, namely, that tides change and tables turn. The present arrangement does not bear the stamp of eternality. Morris reports a warning given by Martin Luther centuries ago:

> God's grace is as a passing storm of rain which does not return where once it has been: It came to the Jews but it passed over; now they have nothing. Paul brought it to the Greeks, but it passed over; the Romans and Latins had it; now they have nothing. You must not think you have it forever.[9]

Of all the communities which comprise the larger ghetto, the black community in America is the most visible. An analysis of this community in terms of its social aberrations is essential to a proper understanding of black needs and aspirations.

FOOTNOTES

1. W. E. Burghardt DuBois, *The Souls of Black Folk,* p. 23.

2. Pierre Jalee, *The Pillage of the Third World,* p. 5.

3. Ibid., p. 3.

4. Ibid., pp. 15-19.

5. Ibid., p. 15.

6. Jean Lacouture, article in *LeMonde* (October 24, 1964), as cited by Pierre Jalee, *The Pillage of the Third World,* pp. 62-63.

7. Colin Morris, *Unyoung–Uncolored–Unpoor.*

8. Ibid., pp. 31-32.

9. Ibid., pp. 149-50.

4

Social Aberrations
in Ghetto Life

LIFE IN THE GHETTO is essentially the same as life on the mainland, for the difference is in degree more than in kind. Behavior patterns on the island of poverty also exist within the larger society; therefore, Kenneth Clark's description of the ghetto applies to the society as a whole:

> The ghetto is ferment, paradox, conflict, and dilemma. Yet within its pervasive pathology exists a surprising human resilience. The ghetto is hope; it is despair; it is churches and bars. It is aspiration for change, and it is apathy. It is vibrancy; it is stagnation. It is courage and it is defeatism. It is cooperation and concern, and it is suspicion, competitiveness, and rejection. It is the surge toward assimilation, and it is alienation and withdrawal within the protective walls of the ghetto.[1]

Substitute the word *mainland* for *ghetto* and the description remains cogent.

The pathology of ghetto life results not from what takes place there, but by its abundance. The ills are endemic. "The dark ghetto is institutionalized pathology; it is chronic, self-perpetuating pathology. . . . Not only is the pathology of the ghetto self-perpetuating, but one kind of pathology breeds another."[2] Therefore, with the larger society as the norm or the standard for acceptable social behavior, the ghetto falls short when measured against the norm. It is the scene of myriad social aberrations, such as cultural abnormalities, perversions, and deviations from the norm. The norm in American society consists basically of the so-called middle-class virtues: work, chastity, sobriety, and honesty. These relate directly to traditional Protestant Pietism, which historically emphasized the saving of souls to the exclusion of the redemption of sinful social structures. Love and justice in such an ethic are utterly subordinate to piety and patriotism. This was the climate and the soil in which the doctrine of laissez-faire capitalism germinated and flowered. The capitalist system is based on competition, which leads inevitably to conflict, and conflict brings on the compromise of absolute values. For example, the justification of slavery in America necessitated an anthropological conclusion: the Negro is less than human. With the end of legal slavery there came no end to the white psychological commitment to the anthropological conclusion. It remained intact in Southern segregation, in Northern discrimination, and in the ghettoization process.

The result is that the ghetto itself is seen by the larger society as one huge aberration, a deviation from the American norm. It is the primary exhibit and the chief certification of inherent black inferiority and white superiority. From a psychological standpoint, whites need the ghetto. It serves to preserve and perpetuate the myth of white superiority which lower and middle-class whites need to prevent them from seeking creative alliance with blacks to deal with the ruling triumvirate. So "The System" views the ghetto as an abnormality, but it needs the "abnormality" to point up its alleged normality. The conclusion is that white is normal and black abnormal. That is sin with a capital *S*, and it leads to sins with a little *s*. In a community rooted and grounded in powerlessness—created, condoned, and controlled from the outside—social aberrations become a normal way of everyday life. Over extended periods of time they might take on a hue of sanctity and respectability.

With "The System's" creation and preservation of the ghetto, the larger society, which derives psychological satisfaction and economic benefits from the ghetto's existence, forfeits its right to be the behavioral norm and the moral standard-bearer. The larger society is morally unfit to judge the ghetto's inhabitants. Therefore, the aberrations that follow are derived from measurement against a higher and purer standard, the ethic of Jesus implicit in His words, "I am come that they might have life, and that they might have it more abundantly."[3]

Physical Aberrations

Physical aberrations include but are not limited to the following: bad housing, crowded living conditions, rats and vermin, abandoned buildings, limited sanitation services, inadequate police protection, a high crime rate, inferior goods, overpricing, drugs, an overabundance of liquor stores, muggings, robberies, police payoffs, numerous fires, lead poisoning, high unemployment, working mothers, idle men, a high incidence of welfare recipients, loan sharks, hunger, malnutrition, inadequate health care, and a high mortality rate for infants and adults.

Psychospiritual Aberrations

Aberrations in the psychospiritual category are the natural byproducts of those in the physical category. They include such conditions as functional illiteracy, hopelessness, apathy, cynicism, broken homes and the resultant trauma, suspicion of others, shattered dreams, and bitter resignation. Written on the forehead of many a ghetto dweller are the words, "I been down so long, till down don't bother me."

Cultural Aberrations

Cultural aberrations stem from the mores, folkways, and belief systems embodied in primary institutions which have either fallen short or utterly failed. Among them are: religious quacks, pimp preachers, prostitutes, nonresident educators, "poverticians," hustlers, con men, distrust of politicians, house niggers, and soul food (the nutritional value of which is seriously questioned).

Economic Aberrations

The ghetto lacks the necessary economic viability to sustain itself. The primary problem is that of the low circulation of capital. Money enters and departs from the ghetto community at an acute angle. There is no known study to substantiate the longevity of a dollar in the ghetto, but Dunbar S. McLaurin, a black economist, put it at about six hours. At that rate, the outgo exceeds the income.

Low wealth spells poor health. In a paper delivered before a Senate Committee on Nutrition and Human Needs on November 3, 1969, Doctors Lester Brestow and Paul Cornley of the American Public Health Association made the following points:

1) The non-White infant mortality rate is twice the White rate.

40

2) Children of families whose income is under $3,000 per year see a Physician 2.6 times per year, while children of families with an income of over $10,000 per year see a Physician 4.4 times per year.

3) Poor families experience three times more heart disease, seven times more visual impairment, and five times more mental disorder.

4) Over 20% of all persons in families of incomes under $3,000 per year have never seen a Dentist.[4]

Health insurance systems in the nation do not relate directly and meaningfully to people of low economic standing. The United States is the only major industrial nation in the world that does not have a national health insurance plan.

Moreover, the ghetto is marked by a sub-economy. U. S. Representative William Clay, Democrat of Missouri, wrote:

> In the ghettos of every major American city there exists a sub-economy. That sub-economy is based on illegal rackets and other underworld activities which flourish in Black communities and are completely acceptable to the white majority. . . . All of this is possible because whites operate this society on a double standard premise. It's based on the racist concept that as long as the actions of Black people only affect the lives of other Black people, it is of no concern to the white power structure.[5]

However, the black sub-economy is not autonomous; it is directed and controlled by the criminal administrators of a super-economy based beyond the perimeter of the ghetto.

Legal Aberrations

The American system of legal justice has always been suspect in the eyes of black people. Such suspicion and distrust are not without foundation. The old Southern system and the more recent "law and order" posture are seen as being directly aimed at the black community. Legal-aid societies are regarded as halfhearted, paternalistic instruments before the legal bar. Court-appointed attorneys are not expected to give fully of themselves in a court of law. Poor police-community relations exist in all major cities. The law represents to whites a friendly helping hand, but to blacks it is a symbol of oppression. Courts are crowded, jails are jammed, and prisons are packed with ghetto inhabitants. It is the general opinion of ghetto people that if a black man steals a television set he is considered a common criminal, while a white man who steals an oil field by deception is considered a financial genius. Legal injustice is a natural postlude to powerlessness.

As a general tendency, whites view the black community in terms of sameness. "All blacks look alike" was for some time a jocular theme. Because of their limited dealings with blacks, most whites sincerely believe that all black people live alike. The ghetto is construed as a great mass of human flesh undifferentiated by social and economic factors. A correction is demanded, for definite social distinctions exist within the black community, where values, life-styles, and attitudes are diverse and varied.

Until the recent psychological revolution with its emphasis on black identity and the beauty of blackness, social distinctions were based on color and capital. Beauty or good looks was related to fairness of complexion, which had a decided influence on one's social standing. The most desired female was "light, bright, and damn near white." The goodness of whiteness was deeply embedded in the black psyche: "If you're white, you're all right; if you're brown, stick around; but if you're black, get back."

As in most cultures, capital also determined social status. Black families of financial standing were admired as status symbols, but black America has never had a class structure analogous to that of white America. The white social structure is highly stratified in terms of caste and class, with factors such as old wealth, blood, and the idea of the nouveau riche figuring prominently in marriage, business, and government. Sociologists have divided the society into divisions of upper class, middle class, and lower class. This kind of socioeconomic arrangement has never been bought by blacks, yet the black community is not devoid of social distinctions. Blacks are certainly not a classless mass. If the typical white categories of caste and class do not apply, how can the social structure of the ghetto be examined and assessed? Dr. Virgil Woods sees the ghetto in terms of "Circles of Entrapment."[6] His division is:

1. The Black Wealthy
2. The Black Street Class
3. The Black Working Class
4. The Black Elite/Middle Class
   (Neo-Colonialist Administrators)
5. The Black Welfare Class
6. The Black Military Class
7. The Black Jail Class

The key word is *circles*, for there are no rungs on a ladder of success. This means that there are interaction, fluidity, and social intercourse; in a word: unity in the midst of diversity. A sense of family is maintained. Between the various circles are links such as kinship, association, religion, political cohesion, and security concerns.

Numerous attempts have been made by "The System" to maintain existing divisions and create new divisions in the black community. Tactics such as "elimination by elevation" have been regularly employed. Many a socially aware, politically sensitive, articulate black, working at the pavement level for the enhancement of the community, has been lifted to a public payroll position in order to dissipate his power and influence. The "War on Poverty" has been a battleground where blacks have been forced to compete for crumbs. The Office of Economic Opportunity's doctrine of "Maximum Feasible Participation of the Poor" has allowed for situation after situation where blacks, unaccustomed to budget financing and unfamiliar with the intricacies of bureaucracy, have had to make policy decisions involving the expenditure of millions of dollars. And when things have gone wrong, they have been made the objects of governmental scorn and community accusation.

Revenue sharing also undercuts the whole idea of a black national thrust and forces each local entity to fight city hall and contend with fellow sufferers for its own survival. Above all of these divisive measures stands "The System," whose agents attempt to create a spirit of ethnocentrism within certain blacks by saying to them, "You're different from the others." The colonizers, located on the mainland, seek continually to bleed the colony of its best minds and energies. An energy drain coupled with a brain drain spells desolation. The question of black survival is crucial. Samuel Yette makes a most pessimistic pronouncement:

> Black Americans have outlived their usefulness. Their raison d'etre to this society has ceased to be a compelling issue. Once an economic asset, they are now considered an economic drag. The wood is all hewn, the water all drawn, the cotton all picked, and the rails reach from coast to coast. The ditches are all dug, the dishes are all put away, and only a few shoes remain to be shined.[7]

According to Yette, blacks have fulfilled their historic

mission: being "hewers of wood and drawers of water," servants of "The System."

Is the oppressor's pathology so deep and great that he would attempt the annihilation of twenty-five million of God's black children? Is his spirit so twisted and perverted that he would seek the elimination of the descendants of blacks on whose backs the nation was built? Colin Morris says of the uncolored:

> Their claim to have educated the Black man is greeted by a hollow laugh. They certainly taught him: they taught him to use a shovel and make them rich; to shin up rubber trees and make them rich. The West did not make the Black man. The Black man made the West.[8]

Can the enormous contributions in art, music, religion, science, and the theater, that which is acknowledged and unacknowledged, be simply dismissed in favor of a genocidal procedure?

Over a quarter of a century ago, in December 1948, the General Assembly of the United Nations adopted unanimously the Convention of the Prevention and Punishment of the Crime of Genocide. The United States government has not yet signed it, but Russia, China, and seventy-three other countries have signed. Morris has little, if any, doubt concerning the moral decadence of the ruling triumvirate:

> They can, at will, reverse the miracle at Cana and turn wine into water. . . . They are so decadent as to make ancient Byzantium seem like the New Jerusalem and yet so decent that even when they are clubbing you to death you feel impelled to apologize for spilling blood on their carpet.[9]

Certain poignant realities must be acknowledged. First, the larger society appears more deeply committed

45

to killing than to healing. This is evidenced in the nation's expenditure of 30 billion dollars per year in the unofficial war in Vietnam and only 2 billion dollars per year in the official war on poverty, and in President Carter's proposed increase in the 1980 defense budget and decrease in proposed expenditure for social service programs. Second, protests by ghetto dwellers against the new colonialism have resulted in pacification rather than elimination. Consequently, the ills grow worse. Third, as Louis S. Smith, president of Operation Bootstrap, pointed out:

> The White man has proven to be a very rational creature on every subject except "race." The nation has never permitted a people of non-White pigmentation to fully participate in every aspect of the society.[10]

America talks with white Communists, but kills yellow Communists. In World War II, 109,000 Japanese-Americans were placed in concentration camps. Similar treatment was not given German-Americans and Italian-Americans, though the nation was at war with Germany and Italy. Only feeble efforts have been made to liberate the black majority in South Africa from the most brutal white oppression. Therefore, a genocidal ethic is not outside the pale of the possible. It may, in fact, be already under way. However, there is no reason to believe that blacks would passively submit to any extermination process. Their pain quotient is too high for them to be fearful of a fight unto death. It may well be that the system which continues to exclude on the basis of color has already written its own postdated death certificate. W. E. B. DuBois made it plain with a question and then an answer:

Have the present masters of the world such an eternal lien on civilization as to ensure unending control? By no means; their very absorption in war and wealth has so weakened their moral fibre that the end of their rule is in sight.[11]

The prophet would add, "The handwriting is on the wall." The nation is "weighed in the balances and found wanting." Even the religion of most white Americans, from the days of slavery to the present era, is inherently racistic.

FOOTNOTES

1. Kenneth B. Clark, *Dark Ghetto,* pp. 11-12.

2. Ibid., p. 81.

3. John 10:10.

4. Lester Brestow and Paul Cornley, paper read before Senate Committee on Nutrition and Human Needs, November 3, 1969, Washington, D. C.

5. William L. Clay, "Economics of Hustling: A Ghetto Blight," *The Boston Globe,* December 21, 1971, p. 31.

6. Virgil Woods, "The Boston Black People's Situation and the Challenge to the Boston Black Community," p. 3.

7. Samuel F. Yette, *The Choice: The Issue of Black Survival in America,* p. 18.

8. Colin Morris, *Unyoung–Uncolored–Unpoor,* p. 61.

9. Ibid., p. 81.

10. Opinion expressed by Louis S. Smith in a lecture at the University of Ghana, July 28, 1972.

11. W. E. Burghardt DuBois, *Color and Democracy,* p. 19.

5

The Involvement
of Racistic Religion

OUR AGE IS MARKED by the abandonment of absolutes. "Graceless moralism" has caused people to turn to secular ethics, which in turn results in "normless relativism."[1] At least three basics have gone into eclipse within the soul-set of the body politic: (1) an authentic belief in and fear of ultimate reality; (2) the belief that "the earth is the Lord's, and the fulness thereof; the world, and they that dwell therein"[2] and (3) the belief in the sanctity of human life. All of these losses, verbiage to the contrary notwithstanding, are visibly apparent in American culture. Irrespective of political mouthings and religious rhetoric, "the tree is known by the fruit it bears." The abandonment of absolutes implies the absence of a genuine theism, which in turn makes for an indisputable demonism.

The Kerner Commission labeled America a racist society. Racism is decidedly more than a sociological abnormality. Racism is demonism—a spiritual perversion! It is the demon that ruined Egypt, Babylon, Greece, Rome, England, and Germany and threatens to destroy America. Racism cannot possibly exist without foundations and underpinnings. To be exact, it requires a doctrine of human nature that in turn produces a value system. In other words, the racist posture is anthropological in its overt expressions and theological in its covert presuppositions. It says something about man and bases it on conclusions regarding the ultimate nature of reality. When stripped to a state of nudity, the racist ascribes to God a posture of partiality predicated on pigmentation, and then assigns to men their permanent places under the sun on the basis of pigmentation. George Kelsey's *Racism and the Christian Understanding of Man* is the most definitive work done to date on this subject. He writes:

> Racist man presumes upon the prerogatives of God. He rejects the divine sovereignty, and requires that God meet his specifications as to nature and purpose. Racism assumes that man has his life at his own disposal, that he can procure his life by his own power. It is life from self rather than from God. It is the final expression of fallen man's confidence that he is by himself and for himself. Thus it is the ultimate sin, for the ultimate sin is the rejection of life as the gift of the Creator, based on the false assumption that life is self-procured.[3]

The racist creates God in his own image, and the creation eventuates in divine racism. Once the scheme is designed and developed, heaven is expected to honor it, angels are asked to applaud it, and white people are called into service by the Eternal to promote and preserve it. Will Herberg describes it:

> In this kind of religion there is no sense of transcendence, no sense of the nothingness of man and his works before

a holy God; in this kind of religion the values of life, and life itself, are not submitted to Almighty God to judge, to shatter, and to reconstruct; on the contrary, life, and the values of life, are given an ultimate sanction by being identified with the divine. In this kind of religion it is not man who serves God, but God who is mobilized and made to serve man and his purposes—whether these purposes be economic prosperity, free enterprise, social reform, democracy, happiness, security, or peace of mind.[4]

So demonic is the diatribe that the iniquity is visited upon the children to all the following generations. Its effective transmission is tremendous testimony to the power of an oral tradition.

In contrast, the Christian Gospel, rooted in the New Testament, holds that to sin against any segment of the human family is to sin against God. To deny or even question another's personhood is sinful. To exclude on the basis of blackness is to call something evil which God has already called good, unless, of course, there is a dichotomy between blackness and humanness. If blacks are nonhuman or even subhuman, whites are guilty of no sin. If blacks are without souls, attitudes of white superiority are not really racist, for all soul-less creatures belong naturally to the realm of animalism. The black man's relationship to God was the cause of serious debate during the early years of American slavery. Questions were raised: Does the slave have a soul? Should the Gospel be preached to slaves? The dilemma was complicated and compounded by the very nature of the servitude. It was chattel slavery. Slaves were primarily property and secondarily persons.

Slavery was basically a Christian enterprise, the first massive program of Christian-sponsored genocide. During the sixteenth and seventeenth centuries, two and one-half million blacks were transported westward to labor on plantations. It is estimated that by the late nineteenth century, fifteen million slaves had been brought alive to the Americas, and that thirty million died in the capturing process and the ordeal of the middle passage.[5] Such a massive program of peddling and killing humans could not have developed without the approval of churches on both sides of the Atlantic. "From the beginning," states Pierre Berton, "it was the Church that put its blessing on slavery and sanctioned a caste system that continues to this day."[6] Being pious religionists, churchmen had to tailor their theology to fit their sociology. Preachers, many of whom were slave-owners, sought to develop a theological justification for the profitable institution of human slavery. The voices that prevailed made a simplistic deduction: Blacks are children of Ham; Ham is forever cursed of God to an existence of servitude; therefore, slavery is of God, the result of a divine decree, and whites are preordained for mastery. But even this perverted interpretation of Scripture did not give a total solution to the problem. No Biblical basis could be found for denying slaves access to the Gospel. Onesimus, a runaway slave, was given the Gospel by the apostle Paul and then sent back to Philemon, his master, not as a slave, but as a brother beloved. Some churchmen contended that converted slaves made better slaves, that they were less hostile and more subservient. The debate subsided, and the slaves had the Gospel preached to them and were baptized into the fellowship of believers.

Black religion, mystical and prophetic even in slavery, predated the black church. Though regarded as chattel, the slaves did not receive the Gospel without critical examination and reflection. Their religious outlook, stemming from the African world view, enabled them to see Jesus Christ as consonant with their traditional un-

derstanding of God. They accepted the Biblical testimony given by the slave masters, but they gave it a
utilitarian twist. With their limited learning, they also saw
clearly the evils of the slave system. They saw the
dichotomy between faith and practice, between Christian
ethics and social policy, and began to demythologize and
personalize the moving stories of Scripture. They read
the Exodus story and started to sing "Pharaoh's Army
Got Drowned One Day." The Negro spirituals were a
prophetic response to a crisis predicament, and they had
both an existential and an eschatological dimension.
They described in forceful language the slave's dreadful
existence, but they also pointed to an ultimate arrangement wherein justice would reign. This arrangement was
expected to come into being on the earth, and it would
certainly be realized in the world to come. The slaves took
the new revelation of God in Christ and created a new
thing, a new salvation history. The parallelisms of the
Israelite experience in Egypt and the black experience in
America were obvious. Blacks considered themselves the
new Israel, and such a self-view called for a new Exodus.

How did slaves look upon the religious foundation
which gave the slave system sanction and support? What
were their attitudes toward white religion? It is clear that
they had the deepest abhorrence for the religion of their
masters. The Reverend Henry Highland Garnet wrote to
slaves in 1848:

> If . . . a band of Christians should attempt to enslave a race
> of heathen men, and to entail slavery upon them and to
> keep them in heathenism in the midst of Christianity, the
> God of Peace would smile upon every effort which the
> injured might make to disenthrall themselves. Brethren,
> it is as wrong for your lordly oppressors to keep you in
> slavery as it was for the man-thief to steal our ancestors
> from the coast of Africa. You should therefore now use

the same manner of resistance as would have been put in our ancestors when the bloody foot-prints of the first remorseless soul-thief were placed upon the doors of our fatherland. The humblest peasant is as free in the sight of God as the proudest monarch that ever swayed a sceptre. Liberty is a spirit sent from God and, like its great Author, is no respecter of persons.[7]

There were some slaves—the Reverend Nat Turner is a striking example—who revolted in the name of the Lord. The slaves were clear in their understanding of where God stood on the question. They also knew that only persons estranged from God could engage in such barbaric behavior. Frederick Douglass, who escaped from slavery in 1838, described his view of the slave master's religion:

We have men-stealers for ministers, women-whippers for missionaries, and cradle-plunderers for church members. The man who wields the blood-clotted cowskin during the week fills the pulpit on Sunday, and claims to be a minister of the meek and lowly Jesus. The man who robs me of my earnings at the end of each week meets me as a class-leader on Sunday morning, to show me the way of life, and the path of salvation. He who sells my sister, for purposes of prostitution, stands forth as the pious advocate of purity. He who proclaims it a religious duty to read the Bible denies me the right of learning to read the name of God who made me. He who is the religious advocate of marriage robs whole millions of its social influences, and leaves them to the ravages of wholesale pollution. The warm defender of the sacredness of the family relation is the same that scatters whole families,—sundering husbands and wives, parents and children, sisters and brothers,—leaving the hut vacant, and the hearth desolate.

They would be shocked at the proposition of fellowshipping a sheep-stealer; and at the same time they hug to their communion a man-stealer, and brand me with

53

being an infidel, if I find fault with them for it. They attend with Pharisaical strictness to the outward forms of religion, and at the same time neglect the weightier matters of the law, judgment, mercy, and faith. . . . They are they who are represented as professing to love God whom they have not seen. They love the heathen on the other side of the globe. They can pray for him, pay money to have the Bible put into his hand, and missionaries to instruct him; while they despise and totally neglect the heathen at their own doors.[8]

In the midst of slavery two separate and distinct views of God and man emerged: the masters' view and the slaves' view; the two were irreconcilable because of the oneness of God's will for His creatures. Black religion and white religion were inherently antithetical. It was only natural that two separate churches—one white and one black—would spring forth out of the rocky soil of human slavery. Racism demands separatism in both church and culture. A segregated society based on a separatist theology resulted in a segregated church. Kyle Haselden is correct: "Long before the little signs—'White Only' and 'Colored Only' appeared in the public utilities, they had appeared in the church."[9] The signs are now gone, but the scars remain; worse still, racism remains a potent presence within the white church.

The white church and white culture are united in unholy wedlock. The similitude is striking. The white church is not free to preach the Gospel because it has not yielded to that Gospel which frees men from pride and sinful presumption. White clergymen, by and large, are puppets instead of prophets; they are allies of the adversary. The white church, historically and presently, is an instrument of "The System," sanctifying its sins, and inspiring its iniquitous deeds. It has never assaulted the prevailing power arrangement in the name of Him who "hath made of one blood all nations of men for to dwell on all the face of the earth."[10] Hence, the nation is in a "Christian" mess, from the White House to the court-house. The primal cause is the Church's "uncertain sound." The four main functions of the Church or the ecclesia are: (1) *kerygma,* (2) *didache,* (3) *diakonia,* and (4) *koinonia.* The white church has failed in all those func-tions. Thus, authentic Christianity has a missionary pur-pose with respect to racist religion. James Cone defines the Church as "that people called into being by the power and love of God to share in his revolutionary activity for the liberation of man."[11] Men, faithful to their Lord's calling, must speak to racistic religion and do so with the truth that sets men free.

One aspect of the truth that liberates is an insistence that certain basic needs be recognized and acknowl-edged. There are three fundamentals with which the white church must come to terms: (1) an understanding of the relationship between love, power, and justice; (2) repentance and reparation; and (3) an awakening to the prophetic function. Let us look at each.

In the first place, love, power, and justice are inextri-cably related. In black-white relations there exists a tre-mendous maldistribution of power. The issue is one of black, powerless conscience versus white, conscienceless power. Kenneth L. Smith and Ira G. Zepp, Jr., are cor-rect when they say:

> Social inequity is the result, not of the failure of religious and rational men to act more lovingly and reasonably, but the possession of an inordinate amount of power by a particular social group or class. The concentration of power in one social group leads to the entrenchment of power, and power automatically gives that group a privileged position and an advantage over other groups.[12]

Lord Acton rightly remarked that "power tends to corrupt and absolute power tends to corrupt absolutely." The white church, by and large, has refused to acknowledge the uses of institutionalized power in the continuing brutalization of blacks. This reality makes clear the white church's failure to understand the dialectical relationship between love and justice. Traditionally, Southern churchmen claimed love without justice while Northern churchmen claimed justice without love. But love without justice is sentimental, and justice without love is tyrannical. One without the other nullifies the existence of both. The truth is that blacks have experienced neither love nor justice in their historic relations with whites.

E. Clinton Gardner, in his *Biblical Faith and Social Ethics,* points out "the widespread tendency to restrict the concern of Christian ethics to personal relationships, and thereby dispense with the demand for justice as a part of Christian ethics."[13] When the Christian ethic is limited to personal relationships, social structures are permitted, by default, to go unmonitored, unaltered, and to remain unredeemed. The vertical dimension of Christian faith is emphasized to the neglect of horizontal responsibility. In other words, both love and justice are severely limited and restricted to a narrow provincialism. "Love in the area of personal relations can never be a substitute for justice in society."[14] Gardner gives three fundamental relationships of love to justice: (1) love is the fulfillment of justice; (2) justice is a necessary instrument of love; and (3) love is for Christians the ultimate norm of justice.[15] Love is the end, and justice is the means by which the end if attained.

Paul Tillich, in stressing the ontology of justice, stated that "ultimately love must satisfy justice in order to be real love, and that justice must be elevated into unity with love in order to avoid the injustice of eternal destruction."[16] The gross inequities in American society clearly reveal that justice has not been satisfied, and that, therefore, real love is nonexistent. Tillich further advises:

> Love reunites; justice preserves what is to be reunited. It is the form in which and through which love performs its work. Justice in its ultimate meaning is creative justice, and creative justice is the form of reuniting love.[17]

White churchmen, if they would be faithful to the Gospel and truly seek the beloved community, must come to terms with the inextricable relationship of love, power, and justice. They must recognize justice as the instrument of love, and power as the instrument of justice. The existing estrangement cannot be overcome in the absence of equity. Reconciliation without justice is impossible, for reconciliation is on the other side of justice. Persons who claim an affinity with Jesus Christ should readily see the implications and demands of the Gospel with respect to social justice. Joseph H. Fichter writes:

> Better than any other institution, organized religion ought to understand the terms of the struggle for racial freedom and equality. Religious-minded people ought to grasp more readily than others such concepts as reparation for wrong-doing, reconciliation of the estranged, resolution for improvement, commitment to values, firm purpose of amendment, fellowship and brotherhood, love and justice.[18]

Second, the white church must exercise repentance and reparation. The elimination of racism from the white psyche requires repentance at the vertical dimension and reparation at the horizontal level. Repentance is generally defined as "godly sorrow for sin with the aim of turning from sin to righteousness." Contrition and penitence are essential ingredients. The ringing declaration made by the prophets in Israel, John the Baptist, Jesus of Nazareth, and the first apostles was "Repent!" The repentance required is due first unto God. It is His creation that has been spoiled; His goodness that has been offended; and His mercy that has been mistreated. What men do to other men is sequential to what they have already done to God. Love of self to the exclusion of love of God leads to love of self to the exclusion of other selves. The gruesome ghetto, circled by racism and racistic religion, declares the white church bloodguilty! The proper, initial response is to say to God, "Against thee . . . have I sinned, and done this evil in thy sight."[19] When repentance is real, reparation follows. Forgiveness by God frees men to perform that which is right.

When James Forman and a few associates in Amos-like manner interrupted the worship service at the Riverside Church in New York City on Sunday, May 4, 1969, cries of outrage echoed throughout Christian America. The idea of a service of worship being disrupted was unthinkable, and a demand for reparations was viewed as utterly absurd. The almost universal negative reaction by whites revealed no appreciation of the centuries of systematic exclusion and deprivation experienced by blacks. Beyond this, whites failed to see themselves as beneficiaries of the racist system. Every child born to white parents enters the world with a decided advantage, and the advantage stays with the child from the cradle to the grave.

However, Ernest Campbell, preaching minister at Riverside Church, understood well the religious significance of Forman's action and his pronouncements. Included in Campbell's written reaction were these statements:

When the church refuses to follow her Lord into the busy throughfares of history, when it talks of love but fails to press for basic justice, when its message has no other focus than the well-being of individual souls and lacks all public reference, when it refuses to put its own power on the line on behalf of the disadvantaged, when it lowers its voice in order to raise its budget, when it becomes more concerned to perpetuate and adorn its life than to lose its life for the sake of Christ and the gospel—when all of this happens, as it has, the church can be rightly charged with contributing to the social and economic inequities that provoke minorities to violence.

The word "reparations" has come up frequently of late. The latest edition of Random House Dictionary gives as the first meaning of the term, "The making of amends for wrong or injury done." From the beginning the Christian Church has taught that restitution is an essential part of penitence. You don't simply say "I'm sorry" to a man you've robbed. You return what you stole or your apology takes on a hollow ring.[20]

White churches, for the sake of their own redemption, must repent and make reparation, and demand the same of the nation as a whole. Zaccheus's example is worthy of emulation: " 'Behold, Lord, the half of my goods I give to the poor; and if I have defrauded any one of anything, I restore it fourfold.' And Jesus said to him, 'Today salvation has come to this house.' "[21] Real repentance will lead to reparation by the white church.

Third, the white church needs to be awakened to the prophetic function. The supreme symbol of the Christian faith is the cross, rough-hewn and blood-soaked, beneath a turbulent sky on a skull-shaped hill, in the midst of cursing men. It is at the cross and through the cross that God intersects the human predicament. At the cross the Church receives its Gospel, a Gospel of judgment and redemption, a Gospel of liberation for captive spirits, a Gospel which offers a new humanity to sinful men. The essence of the Gospel is creative conflict for the purpose of conciliation. The Kingdom of God is consistently at variance with the kingdoms of this world. The prophetic function, therefore, is one of continual confrontation with any and all forces inimical to the abundant life for all men. Tillich rightly stated that "in its prophetic role the Church is the guardian who reveals dynamic structures in society and undercuts their demonic power by revealing them, even within the Church itself."[22]

The prophetic function is fundamentally that of cross-bearing, which may well include being scarred, having to bleed, and perhaps even dying. Said Dietrich Bonhoeffer:

> Suffering . . . is the badge of true discipleship. The disciple is not above his master. Following Christ means *passio passiva*, suffering because we have to suffer. . . . If we refuse to take up our cross and submit to suffering and rejection at the hands of men, we forfeit our fellowship with Christ and have ceased to follow him.[23]

Essential to the carrying out of the prophetic function is a proper allegiance—to say with Peter before the tribunal, "We must obey God rather than men."[24] Such a stance may bring on a crucifixion, but without a crucifixion there can be no resurrection.

The ghetto is a creation of white America with its racist religion. It is to the larger society what the isle of Patmos was to the mainland. On the island are the slaves to the empire. Some of them, like John, have been in the spirit on the Lord's day. They have a message for the church on the mainland. It reads:

> I know your works: you are neither cold nor hot. Would that you were cold or hot! So, because you are lukewarm, and neither cold nor hot, I will spew you out of my mouth. For you say, I am rich, I have prospered, and I

need nothing; not knowing that you are wretched, pitiable, poor, blind, and naked. Therefore I counsel you to buy from me gold refined by fire, that you may be rich, and white garments to clothe you and to keep the shame of your nakedness from being seen, and salve to anoint your eyes, that you may see. Those whom I love, I reprove and chasten; so be zealous and repent.[25]

Lukewarm religion leaves the Church wretched, miserable, poor, blind, and naked, deserving of death but ready for redemption. And redemption always begins with repentance. When repentance does not occur, divine activity in behalf of the victims is in no wise halted, for the Biblical record reveals that God is always on the side of the disinherited. He is the God of the ghetto!

FOOTNOTES

1. Paul Tillich, *Morality and Beyond*, p. 14.

2. Psalm 24:1.

3. George D. Kelsey, *Racism and the Christian Understanding of Man*, p. 146.

4. Will Herberg, *Protestant, Catholic, and Jew*, p. 285.

5. Arnold Schuchter, *Reparations*, p. 45.

6. Pierre Berton, *The Comfortable Pew*, p. 29.

7. Henry Highland Garnet, as quoted in Benjamin E. Mays, *The Negro's God*, p. 46.

8. Frederick Douglass, as quoted in Arnold Schuchter, *Reparations*, pp. 223-34.

9. Kyle Haselden, *The Racial Problem in Christian Perspective*, p. 29.

10. Acts 17:18.

11. James H. Cone, *Black Theology and Black Power*, p. 63.

12. Kenneth L. Smith and Ira G. Zepp, Jr., *Search for the Beloved Community: The Thinking of Martin Luther King, Jr.*, p. 82.

13. E. Clinton Gardner, *Biblical Faith and Social Ethics*, p. 262.

14. Ibid.

15. Ibid., pp. 262-70.

16. Paul Tillich, *Love, Power, and Justice*, p. 14.

17. Ibid., p. 71.

18. Joseph H. Fichter, "American Religion and the Negro," *Daedalus* 94 (1965): 1085.

19. Psalm 51:4.

20. Ernest T. Campbell, quoted in *Tempo*, June 1, 1969.

21. Luke 19:8-9 (RSV).

22. Paul Tillich, *Theology of Culture*, p. 50.

23. Dietrich Bonhoeffer, *The Cost of Discipleship*, pp. 100-101.

24. Acts 5:29 (RSV).

25. Revelation 3:15-19 (RSV).

6

God and the Ghetto

ON THE OUTSIDE WALL OF A CATHEDRAL in Barcelona, Spain, there is a bronze plaque with an interesting engraving. It is a scale, a pair of balances, with an eagle on one side and a turtle on the other. Upon seeing it, I inquired of my guide, "What is the symbolism? What does it mean?" He answered, "It is a symbol of justice. Justice should be as swift as an eagle, but it's as slow as a turtle." Such a statement at once leads the mind of a black American not to some political theory or philosophical treatment of the idea of justice, but to America and the American dilemma, the American promise yet unhonored. In a quick moment, the years are traversed and the mind races back to the period of slavery with its agony and affliction. Segregation, discrimination, the struggle for basic freedoms, the sweat, the tears, and the blood—all of these come into focus, seemingly at once.

GOD IN THE GHETTO

The history of humankind, from Eden's flaming gate to the iron curtain, and on to the bloody battlefields of either side of the bamboo curtain, is a catalog listing the sins of man against his fellowman. Injustice is tragically akin to the human pilgrimage. It occurs regularly in private instances. There, personal injury results. But its most severe consequences are seen in collective instances where one group suffers abuse at the hand of another group. In such cases it almost always emerges from the desensitized consciences of people who deem themselves better than others. It is the Pharaoh ideology at work. Pharaoh is the historic prototype of practitioners of the art of human control. The Israelite experience in Egypt has come to be a frame of reference for all peoples that suffer under the yoke of oppression. The Egyptian experiment has for its historical companions such examples as the slave situation in America and the Jewish holocaust in Nazi Germany. It was a program of massive persecution. The components included forced labor and hard taskmasters, with genocide as the ultimate solution.

The chief problem with the Pharaoh ideology is its mockery of the doctrine of creation. It presupposes a theology that begins with a Creator whose concern is limited. Over against the idea of the absolute sovereignty of God, the master-race concept always eventuates in a posture of rivalry with God. Man was made not to compete but to cooperate with God. In the Egyptian-Israelite situation, the doctrine of ethical monotheism germinated and began to bloom. God placed His power on the side of the oppressed. In an hour of moral and ethical insanity, when the Nile became the watery grave of innocent Hebrew boys, God moved. The very river which Pharaoh had chosen for death was selected by God for deliverance. He saved Moses' life and arranged for him to be reared in Pharaoh's house with Jochebed, his mother, as his nurse. Though born of slave parents in a mud hut on the bank of the Nile, with the threat of death upon him, Moses was God's instrument to give birth to a nation. Raised and nurtured in the ways of the Egyptians, he did not forget that his basic affinity was with the captive community. When he came of age, he went out unto his brethren. Given the choice between a position of power in Egypt and life with a despised and persecuted people, he chose the latter. And when the call was given by God for him to move from shepherdship to leadership, God's view of the ghetto predicament in ancient Egypt was clearly revealed. God said to Moses:

> Go and gather the elders of Israel together, and say to them, "The Lord, the God of your fathers, the God of Abraham, of Isaac, and of Jacob, has appeared to me saying, 'I have observed you and what has been done to you in Egypt; and I promise that I will bring you up out of the affliction of Egypt, to . . . a land flowing with milk and honey.' "[1]

The Exodus was an experience of total emancipation, the movement of a nation within a nation out of bondage into a land promised and provided by God. However, sin is without racial boundaries. There is no positive correlation between sin and skin. The evils of caste and class that victimized Israel in Egypt developed within the Israelite community in their own land. The prophetic writings of the Old Testament deal primarily with the problems precipitated by sin within the covenant community.

The ethical demands of true religion come into sharpest focus in the preaching of the eighth-century prophets, of whom Amos of Tekoa was the foremost spokesman. Regarding the political and religious situation at the time, Charles Kent wrote:

> The task of Amos and his fellow prophets was rendered doubly difficult by the fact that Northern Israel was then

at the height of its national prosperity. Victories and wealth were regarded as convincing proof that the nation enjoyed in a unique degree Jehovah's approval. The lavish gifts and elaborate ritual at the national sanctuary satisfied the national conscience and furnished the insecure basis for the prevailing optimism. This false confidence so blinded the eyes of Israel's leaders that they failed to appreciate the ominous significance of the steady approach of the invincible Assyrian armies. Social injustice was strongly intrenched in temple as well as in palace.[2]

Amos directed his message to the powerful and the privileged. For him there was no dichotomy between the political and religious spheres; all of life was sacred. Any violation of the sanctity of life was an affront to Jehovah. Therefore, Jehovah was the complainant:

> Publish in the palaces at Ashdod,
> and in the palaces in the land of Egypt,
> and say, Assemble yourselves upon the mountains
> of Samaria, and behold the great tumults in the
> midst thereof.
> For they know not to do right, saith the Lord,
> who store up violence and robbery in their palaces.[3]

The positive principle underlying the prophet's stern judgment is that the first duty of rulers is to protect jealously and valiantly the rights of the poor and defenseless. Amos was especially alarmed and aroused by the groundless optimism of the rulers of both Judah and Israel:

> Woe to them that are at ease in Zion,
> and trust in the mountain of Samaria,

which are named chief of the nations,
to whom the house of Israel came!
Pass ye unto Calneh, and see; and from
thence go ye to Hamath the great: then
go down to Gath of the Philistines: be
they better than these kingdoms? or their
border greater than your border?
Ye that put far away the evil day, and
cause the seat of violence to come near;
That lie upon beds of ivory, and stretch
themselves upon their couches, and eat the
lambs out of the flock, and the calves out
of the midst of the stall;
That chant to the sound of the viol, and
invent to themselves instruments of musick,
like David;
That drink wine in bowls, and anoint themselves
with the chief ointments: but they are not
grieved for the affliction of Joseph.[4]

Democracy and justice, under God, are the two central themes in Amos's teachings. The national ideal is that arrangement whereby, in response to the justice and holiness of God, human justice rolls "down like waters, and righteousness like an everflowing stream."[5] The revelation of God which came to the people of Israel had as its primal purpose the rule of God in human affairs.

The public ethic of Jesus of Nazareth validated the prophetic message of the Old Covenant. The purpose of the Incarnation was to demonstrate in history that God loves the world and that religion should serve the physical and spiritual needs of people. The nature of the Messianic mission was made unequivocally clear when Jesus stood in the synagogue in Nazareth and read from Isaiah:

> The Spirit of the Lord is upon me, because he has anointed me to preach good news to the poor. He has sent me to proclaim release to the captives and recovering of sight to the blind, to set at liberty those who are oppressed, to proclaim the acceptable year of the Lord. . . . Today this scripture has been fulfilled in your hearing.[6]

Jesus came to declare the presence of God everywhere. No situation was deemed off limits to the sacred presence. He was Deity incarnate and the Friend of sinners. He taught that the vertical relationship is not marred by horizontal movements among people, regardless of their sin or their human condition. The Good News He brought was that religion is for people. He brought God to dusty roads and back streets, and He voiced God's concern about all human conditions detrimental to the abundant life. Wherever He went, from Capernaum to Calvary, He was engaged in fellowship with the forgotten and showed love for the least.

The Church which He founded was expected to be the extension of His own incarnation, the salt of the earth and the light of the world. As Karl Barth has written,

> The Church is witness to the fact that the Son of man came to seek and to save the lost. And this implies that— casting all false impartiality aside—the Church must concentrate first on the lower and lowest levels of human society. The poor, the socially and economically weak and threatened will always be the object of its primary and particular concern, and it will always insist on the State's special responsibility for these weaker members of society.[7]

How has the Church fared in fulfilling its primary mission to ghetto dwellers? The emphasis, unfortunately, has been mainly that of presenting Jesus as the Son of God instead of the Son of man. Almost always He referred to Himself as the Son of man. But the Church has presented Him in celestial colors and royal regalia which He did not request or desire. In stressing His divinity, the Church has nearly forgotten His humanity. Calvary is remembered while Bethlehem is forgotten. He lived among men before dying for men. But even in the Calvary event, divine love expressed itself through the greatest human concern: "Greater love hath no man than this, that a man lay down his life for his friends."[8]

After nearly twenty centuries, confusion still persists on the question of the Church's mission. Churchmen en masse have yet to capture the impact of Jesus' reply to John the Baptist's query, "Are you he who is to come, or shall we look for another?" Jesus's answer was clear and direct:

> Go and tell John what you hear and see: the blind receive their sight and the lame walk, lepers are cleansed and the deaf hear, and the dead are raised up, and the poor have good news preached to them.[9]

The sum and substance of the reply was that Jesus was involved in a people's program. The emphasis was not centered in pulpit or pew, but in the public square where sin and sickness abounded. Bonhoeffer made a serious point when he said:

> The followers are a visible community . . . Flight into the invisible is a denial of the call. A community of Jesus which seeks to hide itself has ceased to follow him.[10]

The Church in America, unfortunately, has a high visibility quotient only with respect to physical church structures. In terms of activistic affliction, the visibility level is minimal. The prevailing position is one of "up with the church and down with the world." This is a living contradiction to the position of Jesus. In His priestly prayer on the night of His betrayal, He said to the Father regarding the disciples:

> I have given them thy word; and the world has hated them because they are not of the world, even as I am not of the world. I do not pray that thou shouldst take them out of the world, but that thou shouldst keep them from the evil one. They are not of the world, even as I am not of the world. Sanctify them in the truth; thy word is truth. As thou didst send me into the world, so I have sent them into the world.[11]

Jesus prayed as a priest that His Church would be prophetic. His petition made no room for a worldless witness. Believers are in the world and of the Church. Monasticism and asceticism are not presented in the Gospel narratives as models for Christian witness. Jesus Himself is the role model for all who claim an affinity with Him. His humanity was thoroughgoing, a humanity that was touched by other humans and tempted by the wiles of the devil. His hometown was the slum section of Galilee. He grew up in a ghetto. He sat and supped with sinners. He and His men went without wallets and lived mainly on handouts. In a real sense, they were on the Galilee welfare rolls. So blighted was the town of His rearing that when Nathaniel first heard of Him, he asked, "Can anything good come out of Nazareth?"[12] His enemies attacked Him for engaging in dialogue with the despised. He answered them by declaring, "Those who are well have no need of a physician, but those who are sick."[13] Not once did He deviate from His announced mission as recorded in Luke 4. His parable of the judgment was a recital of the same ethic:

> Then the King will say to those at his right hand, "Come, O blessed of my Father, inherit the kingdom prepared for you from the foundation of the world; for I was

hungry and you gave me food, I was thirsty and you gave
me drink, I was a stranger and you welcomed me, I was
naked and you clothed me, I was sick and you visited me,
I was in prison and you came to see me." Then the
righteous will answer him, "Lord, when did we see thee
hungry and feed thee, or thirsty and give thee drink?
And when did we see thee a stranger and welcome thee,
or naked and clothe thee? And when did we see thee sick
or in prison and visit thee?" And the King will answer
them, "Truly, I say to you, as you did it to one of the least
of these, my brethren, you did it to me."[14]

Final judgment is based on a fundamental sensitivity to
human need that ushers forth in creative behavior which
has as its only purpose the healing of men's hurt. Whatever is done to people is done to God. Jesus the Christ
travels incognito along every human pathway. He is the
stranger at the gate, the beggar at the door, and the
ghetto dweller. He is ever present in people. Recognition
of this reality is the vision He requires of His Church.

The apostle Paul has been called by some the co-
founder of Christianity. Conversant with the various cultures of his day, Paul, after his dramatic conversion to the
Christian faith, launched the Church's first extensive
missionary program. In his establishment of the church
at Philippi, the westward march of Christianity was be-
gun. His writings, when examined in totality, reveal a
profound distaste for provincialism and a sweeping, universal concern. The universe was "one verse." The family
of man was one. On Mars' Hill, in the city of Athens, the
seat of Grecian affairs and cradle of philosophic inquiry,
Paul assaulted any and all philosophies of history predicated on a notion of divine favoritism. He said, God "hath
made of one blood all nations of men for to dwell on all
the face of the earth."[15] His universal perspective is
echoed in his Epistle to the Romans: "For there is no
difference between the Jew and the Greek: for the same

Lord over all is rich unto all that call upon him."[16] Race, for Paul, was not a Christian category. No segment of the human family had a corner on God's grace. The basics of biology and the tenets of theology were on the same continuum.

The idea of a racial church was unthinkable to the tentmaker from Tarsus. Christ was not divided, nor was He a divider of men. The purpose of His redemptive activity was to reestablish man's relationship with God, and man's relationship with man by the blood of the everlasting covenant. The Church was to be the earthly expression of the unity or oneness of God's purpose. Paul wrote to Christians in the church at Ephesus:

> Now therefore ye are no more strangers and foreigners, but fellow-citizens with the saints, and of the household of God; and are built upon the foundation of the apostles and prophets, Jesus Christ himself being the chief corner stone; in whom all the building fitly framed together groweth unto an holy temple in the Lord: in whom ye also are builded together for an habitation of God through the Spirit.[17]

One family, under one God, constituting one Church was the Pauline position with respect to the Christian ideal.

However, the reality that Paul saw presented a strikingly different picture. When he studied the human response to the revelation of God in Christ, he saw that God's best reception was taking place among those caught in the throes of the ghetto predicament. The comment made about Jesus' ministry, "The common people heard him gladly,"[18] was a continuing reality. In his first missive to the Corinthian Christians, Paul wrote:

> For ye see your calling, brethren, how that not many wise men after the flesh, not many mighty, not many noble,

are called; but God hath chosen the foolish things of the world to confound the wise; and God hath chosen the weak things of the world to confound the things which are mighty.[19]

This is a jarring declaration to Christians of a culture-oriented church that has always said implicitly that God's best belongs to the so-called better people who reside in the better communities.

The white church has declared by its deeds that God's primary presence is outside the perimeter of poverty and its attending pain, and that if one desires to call upon God at His chief residence, one must travel beyond the din and dither of the struggling masses. By misreading God's humanity, the white church has missed His humility. Paul's words indict so much that so many have made so sacred. The above passage from Paul's first letter to the church at Corinth is out of place in many pulpits. Clarence Jordan's Cotton Patch rendering is more piercing:

> Very few of your members are highly educated, not many are influential or from the upper crust. It appears as though God deliberately selected the world's "morons" to show up the wise guys, and the world's weaklings to show up the high and mighty, and the world's lowly and rejected—the nobodies—to put the heat on the some-bodies.[20]

If this were an isolated passage, some comfort would be afforded the privileged. But it does not exist in Scriptural solitude; rather, it is the very warp and woof of the New Testament. It is a capsule chronicle of the Master's ministry. Paul's pointed pronouncement could not possibly be the Pentagon's favorite passage. It is totally alien to Wall Street and Madison Avenue. "Not many wise . . . not many mighty . . . not many noble, are called." Some wise, some mighty, some noble, but not many! Only a few! The things men honor most—the colossal, the stupendous, the spectacular—enjoy no particular favor with God. Paul says that the holy Presence is most pronounced at a lower level, down at the bottom with the foolish, the weak, the base, and the despised. The best word for that characterization is *ghetto.*

The written record of God's revelation to man gives no moral sanction to the political princes who preside over unjust human systems. God's agenda is not written in decadent capitals. His platform is not developed by money barons whose interest in people is abrogated by their pursuit of profits. It appears not accidental that while the Greeks were delving in philosophy, while the Romans were conquering the world, and while certain Jews were corrupting religion, God was on His way to a stable in Bethlehem. God's strategy of human redemption works not from the top down, but from the bottom up. The political process is not synonymous with the divine strategy. Always with God, the victimizers are under judgment, while the victims are under mercy. More profoundly then anywhere else, God is at work in the low places of existence. He is God of the ghetto, for in the groanings of the ghetto there is the quest for God, His truth, His goodness, and His liberating power. Those who exist under the heel of human tyranny and at the same time keep alive the vision of their God-appointed destiny are co-workers with God in the task of confronting the system.

FOOTNOTES

1. Exodus 3:16-17 (RSV).

2. Charles Foster Kent, *The Social Teachings of the Prophets and Jesus,* p. 40.

3. Amos 3:9-10 (KJV).

4. Amos 6:1, 3-6 (KJV).

5. Amos 5:24 (RSV).

6. Luke 4:18-21.

7. Karl Barth, *Community, State, and Church,* p. 173.

8. John 15:13.

9. Matthew 11:3-5 (RSV).

10. Dietrich aeanhoeffer, *The Cost of Discipleship,* p. 132.

11. John 17:14-18 (RSV).

12. John 1:46 (RSV).

13. Luke 5:31 (RSV).

14. Matthew 25:34-40 (RSV).

15. Acts 17:26.

16. Romans 10:12.

17. Ephesians 2:19-22.

18. Mark 12:37.

19. I Cor. 1:26-27.

20. Clarence Jordan, *The Cotton Patch Version of Paul's Epistles,* p. 48.

7

Confronting the System

THERE ARE ESSENTIALLY THREE WAYS to look at the American System. One is through the lenses of telescopic idealism. This sometimes results in a view of American culture as the new Eldorado, and evokes intense feelings about the manifest destiny of America. It often leads to political messianism, as witnessed in the often-stated remarks about America's duty to "make the world safe for democracy." The rationale for American involvement in both the Korean War and the war in Vietnam was repeatedly expressed in these terms. America is continually lifted up by her political representatives as "the leader of the free world." Ironically, the so-called free world is composed of that segment of the white world which exercises its power to dominate the rest of the world. Furthermore, the leaders of the nations which make up the "free world" have never agreed that America is indeed their leader. Charles P. Hamilton, Jr.'s book *The*

Nixon Theology is a clear commentary on civil religion in America and its attending spirit of ethnocentrism. Commenting on former President Richard M. Nixon's reaction to the Apollo moonshot, Hamilton reports:

> In his euphoria following the splashdown, the President had said to a group of foreign students: "Any culture which can put a man on the moon is capable of fathering all nations of the earth in peace, justice and concord." In addition to the lapse of diplomacy involved in making such a chauvinistic statement in the presence of foreigners, Nixon's remark betrayed one of his most critical weaknesses. He seems so certain that the values of this country are universally binding that he could find even in the technological success of a moonshot the symbol of a transcendent mission.[1]

Telescopic idealism is at best replete with fantasy and mythomania. America is not the Kingdom of God on earth.

Telescopic idealism is also reflected in the nation's posture of economic messianism. The inscription on the base of the Statue of Liberty is a clear example:

> "Keep, ancient land, your storied pomp!" cries she
> with silent lips. "Give me your tired, your poor,
> your huddled masses yearning to be free,
> the wretched refuse of your teeming shore,
> send them, the homeless, the tempest-tossed to me,
> I lift my lamp beside the golden door."

Messianic notions have resulted in the widespread attitude, even in pulpit and pew, that government policies and actions should not be subjected to sharp criticism and harsh judgment. The late Cardinal Spellman often declared: "My country, right or wrong." Others have repeatedly echoed his pronouncement in myriad ways.

From a Christian perspective, an attitude of moral superiority over other nations vitiates any good that is done for the suffering peoples of the world.

A second way to view the nation is through the lenses of microscopic realism. This view can eventuate in a characterization of the nation as the seat of satanic power, hell on earth, and the perfect embodiment of the demonic. Those in this camp run the gamut from cynicism to nihilism.

The third approach is one of holding telescopic idealism and microscopic realism in a state of dialectical tension. This view recognizes and acknowledges the nation's virtues and its vices, its grandeur and its wretchedness. To do this is to be faithful to the prophetic function, to see the human order both as it should be, and as it actually is. The prophet is one who has seen "the vision splendid," and then gauges and addresses the human order on the basis of that vision.

A close scrutiny of "The System" reveals that Americans are controlled and manipulated by a sinful minority that is neither young, colored, nor poor. They own the nation's wealth, rape the world's resources, make the political decisions, plan the nation's military ventures, hurt our humanity, and deface our divinity. Ferdinand Lundberg, in his exhaustive study titled *The Rich and the Super-Rich*, points out that the economic and political control of America is in the hands of a highly privileged few:

> . . . 1.6 percent of the adult population own at least 32 percent of all assets, and nearly all the investment assets, and . . . 11 percent of households . . . own 56 percent of the assets and 60 percent of the net worth. It is even possible that 1/2 of 1 percent own more than one-third of all productive assets as of 1965-67. It is evident that this leaves very little to be apportioned among 90 percent of the population.[2]

Lundberg further advises that "most of the productive activity of the United States is in the hands of a tiny number of very large corporations largely owned and completely dominated by a small coterie, almost a junta."[3] Their influence over the decision-making process of the government is tremendous. They are a tightly knit group of men who not only work together through interlocking corporate boards, but who also socialize together for purposes that are ultimately economic and political.

> Not only are the big deals arranged in the comfortable privacy of the interlocking clubs ... but ... general policy governing the interlocking corporate world, as distinct from the specific policy of each company, is there determined. Even big tycoons must eat; and they eat together in their clubs. As it happens, during the meals, arrangements are made for organizing the world after their heart's desires.[4]

The influence of big business in the political sphere is pointedly described by C. Wright Mills in his book *The Power Elite*. According to Mills, the military-industrial complex is controlled by "the inner core of the power elite."

> Each member of the power elite need not be a man who personally decides every decision that is to be ascribed to the power elite. Each member, in the decisions he does make, takes the others seriously into account. They not only make decisions in the several major areas of war and peace; they are the men who, in decisions in which they take no direct part, are taken into decisive account by those who are directly in charge.[5]

Most Americans, prior to the Watergate era, sincerely believed that the nation's affairs were directed by men in government who were free from the pressures of powerful economic interests. Had they listened, they would have learned a serious lesson from Senator Russell Long's admission in a 1967 speech before the United States Senate. The Senator from Louisiana said:

> Most campaign money comes from businessmen. Labor contributions have been greatly exaggerated. It would be my guess that about 95 percent of campaign funds at the congressional level are derived from businessmen. At least 80 percent of this comes from men who could sign a net worth statement exceeding a quarter of a million dollars. . . . Merely by assiduously tending to the problem of business interests located in one's own state, a legislator can generally assure himself of enough financial support to campaign effectively for reelection.[6]

The translation of economic power into political power is part and parcel of "the American way of life." By this process the interests of *the powerful few* are preserved and enhanced, while that which accrues to the well-being of *the powerless many* is almost accidental.

The actual (though unannounced) objective of the ruling triumvirate is to hold on to its power. Total control of the society is implicit in every decision and in every action. They control the systems of communication, define terms, put word labels on all forms of human behavior, and through skillful psychological manipulation, perpetuate and escalate already existing divisions and polarizations. By the use of linguistic devices, they cause certain words to generate terrible fears in most members of the larger society. For example, the words *liberal* and *radical* at one time were considered dirty words. For they applied, in the eyes of most Americans, to persons who were traitors to the best interests of the nation. In recent times, the words *militant* and *revolutionary* hold the preeminence as dirty words. They are distasteful for they are associated with the idea of the overthrowing of the existing governmental order.

To speak of revolution is to disturb domestic tranquility and threaten an already shaky sense of security. But there are some things, like them or not, that are part and parcel of the human pilgrimage. Revolution, in spite of its poignant, piercing character, falls into this category. It touches down not as some new bolt out of the blue. It is as ancient as man's initial estrangement, and stretches across the total mileage of man's marchings. Unlike *evolution,* which connotes gradual change, *revolution* is abrupt, and it involves the overthrowing of the established order rather than the development of its latent capacities for good.

About five centuries before Christ, Aristotle attempted in his *Politics* an explanation of the revolutionary posture in the human situation. "The universal and chief cause of this revolutionary feeling," according to Aristotle, is "the desire of equality, when men think that they are equal to others who have more than themselves."[7] The revolutionary spirit is rooted in the desire to be free, to experience and to enjoy equity, and it is grounded in certain ineluctable urgings of the human spirit. Men bound by oppressive brethren cry out, "I want to be free. Something deep, down within me—that mysterious something called 'the soul'—prods and pushes me, and demands of me that I break out of any unjust confinement to which sinful mortals subject me. Something good and God-like in me rebels and revolts against any and all forms of tyranny." Regardless of any derogatory interpretation given to the revolutionary spirit by the up-people, a genuine thrust toward personhood and/or peoplehood should be regarded as sacred. Victims of tyranny who refuse to acknowledge and actively work for the fulfillment of their God-intended destiny as real persons do violence to the sanctity of their own creation.

In the present world order, freedom is so rare and

81

oppression so common that revolution is commonplace. Deep rumblings and uprooting social convulsions are the order of the day. From nearly every quarter there comes the word of uprisings against human powers that have become demonic. Youths are rebelling against military madness and morally bankrupt value systems. Blacks are revolting against the democratic myth and the plantation ethic. Almost everywhere, there is a rolling tide of resentment toward hindrances and obstacles to human existence. A generation, in some ways new and novel, has come into being. They often speak in rough and abrasive manner; their words are cutting and callous; the language is often crude and unpolished.

The fundamental issue, however, concerns the groanings beneath the linguistics. Are the groanings legitimate? That is the question, for the divine ear is ever alert to the cries of the afflicted. Those who groan, in this writer's view, are on the side of righteousness and make company with the Eternal. In our world, right and righteousness constitute a revolutionary posture. Wrong is so prominent and pervasive that it appears right to be wrong. Those who deem it their duty to challenge the emissaries of evil are relegated to the status of renegades, and the most bitter scorn is reserved for those who seek justice. The most vicious attacks are leveled at persons who strive to be actively Christian.

Against the backdrop of structured sin and institutionalized iniquity, righteousness is thus inherently revolutionary. If one is faithful to the Gospel, one is revolutionary by definition. Arnold Schuchter states the case well:

> For the revolutionary Christian, the message is that the future is his prime responsibility—to subject the earth and its institutions to human welfare, to build truly

human communities of men as the physical and social context of that welfare, and to develop the potential of individuals within those communities to their fullest fruition. Obstacles that stand in the way of carrying out this responsibility are sins which should be removed. This is a vision of redress that has the kind of catalytic power requisite to revolutionary movements. It is a vision of the good society where the many will be favored over the few or the few will not be exploited or oppressed by the many.[8]

The things that belong to God are in such radical opposition to the human order as presently structured that God can be called without apology, "God, the Revolutionary."

The paramount question, historically and presently, centers on the methodology for dealing with the demonic. The writers of the Declaration of Independence recognized clearly the sanctity of revolution and declared forthrightly

that whenever any Form of Government becomes destructive of these Ends, it is the Right of the People to alter or to abolish it, and to institute new Government, laying its Foundation on such Principles, and organizing its Powers in such Form, as to them shall seem most likely to effect their Safety and Happiness.... But when a long Train of Abuses and Usurpations, pursuing invariably the same Object, evinces a Design to reduce them under absolute Despotism, it is their Right, it is their Duty, to throw off such Government, and to provide new Guards for their future Security.[9]

But how does an afflicted minority exercise this right and this duty? Acceptance of its rightness does not necessarily prescribe the method. Morris describes the great need of revolution and the point at which most churchmen put on the brakes:

Nothing short of revolution will cauterize the stinking sores of the West. A fair slice of the Christian world is agreed about that—the Vatican, the World Council of Churches, bishops, theologians, and parish pump preachers. By revolution they mean many things, all important; drastic reform of the Church, more dynamic Christian witness, a new spirit in men's hearts—but they do not mean blood, bombs, and barricades.[10]

The question of method is basically the question of the moral status of violence versus nonviolence. Christians can be observed operating on both sides of the spectrum, with each side affirming its faithfulness to the Gospel. Some embrace an ethic of violent revolution. Others preach a gospel of nonviolent revolution. The latter position is sometimes charged with being a middle-class phenomenon, embraced for security reasons by those who have something to lose. The foremost modern proponent of the nonviolent ethic was the late Martin Luther King, Jr., and yet it is difficult to place the label of absolute pacifism upon him. He said often that Hitler should have been fought because of the demonic nature of his deeds. And, of course, King did not refuse armed protection of himself by others. Emil Brunner's dictum is valid: "He who affirms the State, affirms violence."[11] This means, in a word, that those who refuse to take up arms may have to be defended by others who will.

In so-called Christian America, the national posture has been consistently contradictory in character. America has presented itself to the world as a peace-loving nation, but is simultaneously regarded by the outside world as a warmonger. The nation has never sought the nonviolent distinction in its foreign involvements, but has always urged nonviolence as the only proper course for aggrieved and afflicted citizens. A hybrid mentality exists, which perhaps explains the preponderance of hypocritical double-talk. Great concern has been voiced in recent years about an emerging ethic of violence in the land. Much of this talk is tied to the black thrust for power. But to treat violence as a new thing is absurd, when just a scant trace of history reveals that violence is closely akin to Americanism. The roots of violence sink deeply in Western culture. America's beginning was on a bloody basis. The land was taken from the Indians by violence; independence was secured by violence; blacks were enslaved by violence; and radical but necessary social change has often been prevented by violence. There is little wonder, then, that the victimized masses, here and elsewhere, have adopted as their motto: "By any means necessary!" Ted R. Gurr, co-author of the report of the National Commission of the Causes and Prevention of Violence, acknowledged the tendency of Americans to dismiss certain hard, historical realities:

> Americans have always been given to a kind of historical amnesia that masks much of their turbulent past. Probably all nations share this tendency to sweeten memories of their past through collective repression, but Americans have probably magnified this process of selective recollection, owing to our historic vision of ourselves as a latter-day chosen people, a new Jerusalem.[12]

Perhaps collective repression of facts pertaining to a violent past is to be expected from the heirs of those who engaged in collective oppression. But it does not spare the heirs the burden of dealing presently with the demands of the descendants of those who were oppressed, and who consider themselves sorely oppressed.

How does one deal with the demonic? Methodologically speaking, to choose absolutely between violence and nonviolence is too simplistic. To embrace either ethic absolutely is to deny or to ignore the relativities of the life situation. Both violence and nonviolence are relative strategies in that both are morally ambiguous. The choice of either is necessitated by the absence of love, which is the only absolute ethic. The absence of love makes for the denial of justice which insures the presence of injustice. Jose Bonino, president of Union Theological Seminary, Buenos Aires, sees the question of violence as "a subordinate and relative question." He explains:

> It is subordinate because it has to do with the "cost" of the desired change—the question of the legitimacy of revolution is not decided on the basis of the legitimacy of violence and vice versa. "Violence" is a cost that must be estimated and pondered in relation to a particular revolutionary situation. It is "relative" because in most revolutionary situations . . . violence is already a fact constitutive of the situations: injustice, slave labor, hunger, and exploitation are forms of violence which must be weighed against the cost of revolutionary violence.[13]

In other words, the methodology for dealing with injustice must be determined by the particular social situation and the degree of demonism therein.

In the course of history there have been instances where violence was redemptive. Prayer and fasting did little to stop Hitler and the Nazi juggernaut. Nonviolence has been, at least to date, the most rational and redemptive strategy for blacks in racist America. But nonviolence appears utterly untenable as a means of dealing a deathblow to the apartheid of Southern Rhodesia and South Africa. The proper response to demonic power at the planetary level has to be determined situationally. The choice is not between purity and impurity; it is between differing degrees of sin. There is no social ethic that does not have to consider the sins of man and the relativities of human history, for every social policy is tainted by sin. Perfection is not possible within history.

There is another dimension to the debate over violence and nonviolence. Without the threat of violence (overt or covert, open or veiled), nonviolence is politically impotent. Martin Luther King, Jr., operated at one end of the continuum; Malcolm X and others operated at the opposite end. The almost total rejection of Malcolm facilitated a certain acceptance of King. The hallmark of nonviolence is its view of redemptive suffering, its activistic affliction endured in pursuit of truth and justice. This brand of behavior is noteworthy in its declaration that a profound relationship exists between the victim and the victimizer. Jacques Ellul argues,

> Only in the light of Jesus Christ's sacrifice of himself can man be compelled to live as man. In following the path appointed by Christ we show the other to himself. Camus understood this; he showed that there is a link between the victim and the executioner, showed how the victim can compel the executioner to become a man by recognizing his victim. Seeing the crucified Christ the Roman centurion said, "Certainly this man was innocent." Seeing Joan of Arc burned at the stake the English captain said, "We have burned a saint." At that moment they became men.[14]

Although a profound relationship does seem to exist between the victim and the victimizer, conversion from brute to man also seems to be the rare exception rather than the general rule. Most butchers remain butchers. Case studies in the black-white experience, where butchers have been changed to brothers, have yet to be released. It must also be acknowledged that most victims of "The System" see the attainment of their freedom as primary, and conversion of the victimizers as secondary or unimportant. Redemptive suffering is not the stated goal of the masses of men. It is the method of the saints who are as rare as righteousness itself. It is the conduct of those whose faith assures them that resurrection follows crucifixion, that funeral is followed by festival, and that Sunday will give answers to Friday's questions. In the final analysis, it is the posture of those who are willing to suffer for righteousness' sake, and who do so believing that they are workers together with God in His revolutionary, leveling process expressed to and through Isaiah:

> Every valley shall be exalted, and every mountain and hill shall be made low: and the crooked shall be made straight, and the rough places plain: and the glory of the Lord shall be revealed, and all flesh shall see it together: for the mouth of the Lord hath spoken it.[15]

To recognize the inadequacies of nonviolence as a strategy does not necessarily lead to the unconditional advocacy of violence as the only strategy. The violent strategy is not a viable one for blacks in America. The system may very well deserve a violent revolution, but there is a fundamental difference between militancy and insanity. Aggrieved and frustrated blacks who urge the use of munitions in an armed assault on evil white structures do not understand the nature of the enemy. America is probably the most pathological killer in the history of the world, and one does not go bear hunting with a switch. It would prove initially suicidal and ultimately genocidal. But over and above this, the inhumanity of whites is not worthy of imitation.

Within the ranks of ghetto dwellers, other voices can be heard. There are those who espouse an ethic of separatism or withdrawal from white society. The rhetoric runs all the way from the creation of a separate black state within the continental limits of the United States to a modern exodus with an unspecified African destination. The separatist position is an understandable

reaction to the failures of integration. Stokley Carmichael speaks for millions of blacks when he declares:

> Integration . . . speaks to the problem of blackness in a
> despicable way. As a goal it has been based on complete
> acceptance of the fact *(sic)* that in order to have a decent
> house or education, blacks must move into a white
> neighborhood or send their children to a white school.
>
> This reinforces, among both black and white, the idea
> that "white" is automatically better and "black" is by defi-
> nition inferior. This is a subterfuge for the maintenance
> of white supremacy.[16]

Integration is generally defined in terms of what is best
for whites, which signals a fundamental absence of integ-
rity. It is a one-way street, more monological than dialog-
ical. It preserves paternalism, even within the churches.
Integration is impossible in any cultural setting where
racism is real to any degree. Separatism, on the other
hand, is impossible, both ontologically and practically.
An interim ethic of black asceticism has already proven
profitable. Blacks have withdrawn psychologically,
spiritually, and even culturally, as witnessed by the widespread interest in black history, black art, black music,
black religion, Afro hairstyles, and African dress. This
has served to diminish significantly the black identity
crisis, and represents an eventful step in the movement
from property to pride to power. Neither integration nor
separatism is the goal of blacks. The dominant desired
goal is that of freedom and equity.

Existence without equity is the plight of blacks
throughout America. It is the major hurdle to be overcome. Passive submission to the status quo is the big
barrier that stands in the way. A spirit of defeatism, born
out of centuries of unfulfilled dreams, pervades the
thinking of millions. The problem with this posture is its

denial of the creative powers of the human spirit. It ascribes permanence to society's sinful structures and says that nothing can be done to reverse the downward spiral. Passive submission says "amen" to Yette's assessment: "Examination of the problem must begin with a single, overpowering socioeconomic condition in the society: black Americans are obsolete people."[17]

However, if the majority of blacks believed that they were in fact an obsolete people, hope would be on an unending holiday. The tremendous flux and ferment evident in the black community are a sure indication that most blacks have not surrendered to a spirit of hopelessness and helplessness. Many blacks continue to "sing the Lord's song in a strange land." Whenever there exists within a people a residue of interest in and enthusiasm about the large possibilities of that people, their powerlessness is not absolute. The simple presence of twenty-five million persons of African descent after centuries of maltreatment, miseducation, and ghetto misery says clearly that blacks have not thrown in the towel. The sheer size of the black population undercuts and vitiates the charge of total powerlessness. There is sufficient power present to obviate the charge of obsolescence. The problem is essentially one of the nonutilization and misuse of power.

The point is that there is sufficient latent power in the black community to provide fuel and fire for a strategy of creative coercion. Such a strategy entails, in simple terms, the proper use of existing power to coerce or force the oppressor into a just relationship with the captive community.

Nonviolent direct action as expressed in the campaigns headed by Martin Luther King, Jr., is a striking example of creative coercion. It resulted in the removal of the legal sanctions of segregation and gave blacks throughout the South free access to the ballot. Beyond these, King's actions raised the vision of blacks throughout the nation to the larger possibilities of creative coercion as a method for achieving economic justice. Creative coercion is a just means to a just end. It is a proven route to equity and power. Its spiritual basis is that of noncooperation with evil, an ethical stance deeply rooted in the Judaeo-Christian tradition. Cooperation with evil is tantamount to an endorsement of evil.

The Biblical narratives cite instance after instance where men were more concerned about the state of their souls than the well-being of their bodies. The Exodus is a shining illustration. During the Babylonian Captivity, Shadrach, Meshach, and Abednego, slaves of the empire, told Nebuchadnezzar: "O king . . . we will not serve thy gods, nor worship the golden image which thou hast set up."[18] They decided that it was better to burn than bow. In the midst of the same enslavement, the prophet Daniel refused to eat the king's meat.[19] Rather than betray their Lord, Peter and the other apostles told the Jewish council: "We ought to obey God rather than men."[20] Paul admonished the Christians in Thessalonica to "abstain from all appearance of evil."[21] Noncooperation with evil is fundamental to the liberation of any people. It is the launching pad for a program of creative coercion, for it affirms personhood and peoplehood. It admits to a dignity which is divinely derived, and it says that no man has the right to attempt its destruction.

Three components are absolutely essential to a meaningful program of creative coercion: (1) transformation of the black leadership class; (2) collectivization of black economic power; and (3) politicization of black numerical strength. Let us look at each.

First, there is an urgent need for a transformation of the black leadership class. Black leadership suffers from serious fragmentation. Division is deep not only between different professional groups but also within the various groups. Group interests and individual ambitions take precedence over the total well-being of blacks in the nation. There is widespread difference of opinion about what the actual goals of blacks should be, and about the strategies that should be implemented for the attainment of just goals.

Daniel Thompson, in his study titled *The Negro Leadership Class,* concluded that there are three types of black leaders: "Uncle Tom," the "racial diplomat," and "the race man."[22]

"Uncle Tom," presently not as prominent as heretofore, existed on a large scale both prior to and during the era of the '60s. He was the liaison person between powerful whites and powerless blacks, and his primary allegiance was always to whites. The dispenser of limited favors to the black community, he was expected to "bow and scrape" before whites to receive pitiable favors. Uncle Tom seemed satisfied with the system of segregation. Fortunately, the mortality rate of Uncle Toms has been exceedingly high during the past decade.

The "racial diplomat" is the spiritual successor to Uncle Tom. Generally better educated and more sophisticated, he also serves a liaison function, but does not see himself in that role. He hugs the illusion that he is operating with whites on a peer basis for the good of his people. He is exhibit "A" in black-white relations, a prominent personage at interracial affairs made up of people who have held back the tide of justice for the past fifty years. The racial diplomat can always be expected to mediate differences between the natives and the rulers, but always in a way that guarantees an outcome amenable to the rulers. In the ghetto, he is called an "oreo": black externally but white internally. His social behavior says to ghetto dwellers that he prefers sipping cocktails with the oppressors to shaking hands with the oppressed.

The "race man" is the rare creature in the black leadership class. Though not a racist, he is the embodiment of racial pride and has absolute distaste for the system. His primary devotion is to his brothers and sisters in tribulation. He begs no favors from the establishment, but demands justice for his people. While the up-people regard him as militant, revolutionary, and a troublemaker, his own people see him as a spokesman for and champion of their cause. The task is one of increasing his tribe by sensitizing the "racial diplomat" to the reality, namely, that the ghetto is basically a cultural condition afflicting all blacks in America, and even throughout the world. Only authentic "race men" can creatively confront a racist world.

Second, black economic power must be collectivized. Many have concluded that the technological revolution has already rendered blacks expendable. The conclusion is utterly false. It is true that blacks have limited production power; blacks are mainly consumers and not producers. Though they are instruments of production, they are not producers in the sense of ownership of the means of production. However, consumers are not a powerless group. In a capitalist system, consumption is ultimately more determinative than production. Production minus consumption equals economic chaos. Black consumption power in America is awesome, not simply because the collective annual earning power of blacks is upwards of seventy billion dollars, but also because of the narrow profit margin at which many American businesses and industries operate. The great majority enjoy a profit figure of less than 10 percent. Most food companies realize less than 3 percent. Given the reality of narrow margins of profit, it is clearly understandable how the slogan "The customer is always right" has come into widespread usage.

What does this mean for blacks who dwell at the base of the economic pyramid? It means that they represent the difference between profit and loss for many mass-consumption industries, and these constitute the very backbone and lifeblood of the nation's economy. In existential terms, blacks can spell the difference between life and death for numerous industries and businesses. How can this reality be exploited for purposes that are morally just and equitable?

The ghetto has been previously described as an island of poverty in the midst of a sea of affluence. The ghetto is marked by economic starvation and stagnation. The outgo exceeds the income. Capital is the missing ingredient. The Japanese in California, when faced with the same problem following World War II, adopted a policy which stipulated that every dollar that entered their community had to pass through the hands of at least four Japanese before departing from their community. Such a strategy would certainly strengthen the economic life of the ghetto and is worthy of emulation.

Beyond this, if the larger business community returned to the black community a share proportionate to what blacks contribute in sales and profits, the status of blacks would be appreciably enhanced. Such a "return" should include equitable employment at all levels; a proper percentage of bank deposits to black banks; a just amount of the advertising budget to black advertising companies and black media concerns; an equitable expenditure of the insurance dollar to black insurance companies and agencies; a proper use of black service companies; and a just portion of the philanthropic dollar to black causes. Although black institutions in these categories do not now exist in sufficient strength to handle such a massive "return," white businesses, on the simple basis of the black contribution, should be made to create and develop new black business institutions.

The regularly recited response to this kind of request is that anything which smacks of a quota system or a percentage arrangement is patently undemocratic. The argument is absurd. The evils are too long-standing and too deeply entrenched for the gap to be bridged by any other means. Historically, free enterprise has meant the freedom to deny fair employment, to ignore the pain of ghetto dwellers, and to exploit the ghetto's meager resources for the economic enhancement of whites. The system has been free to be undemocratic in its distribution of power. Powerful economic institutions cannot be expected to move volitionally toward equity. They must be creatively coerced.

The Reverend Richard Allen, founder of the African Methodist Episcopal Church, recognized the necessity of a program of creative coercion more than a century ago. Charles H. Wesley described it as follows:

> Richard Allen was active in the organization of a "Free Produce Society" of Philadelphia. The object of this organization was the purchase of produce grown by free labor only. Its members pledged themselves to make purchases only from merchants who refused to sell slave labor produce. This society grew out of an assembly of colored people at "Richard Allen's Church" on December 20, 1830. About five hundred persons assembled "to form an association to encourage the use of the productions of free laborers in preference to those of slaves."[23]

Allen's methodology was at once that of selective buying and creative coercion.

Two movements in this area have been attempted in recent years. The first was called Selective Patronage, a Philadelphia-based program spearheaded by black clergymen to secure jobs for blacks. The procedure was simple and direct. A minister's committee with an un-named chairman would wait on the head of a major company and present specific job demands. If the company did not favorably respond within a specified time period, four hundred preachers would go to their pulpits and urge their congregants to cease patronizing the company in question. Selective Patronage resulted in many new jobs for Philadelphia blacks, and in the early '60s gave birth to Opportunities Industrialization Centers (OIC), a national and international job-training and job-development program, headed by the Reverend Leon H. Sullivan. The selective patronage concept caught the eye of Martin Luther King's Southern Christian Leadership Conference, and a new program under SCLC auspices was born. Headed initially by the Reverend Jesse Jackson, it took the name Operation Breadbasket. The selective patronage concept was expanded beyond demands for jobs, to include banking, insurance, advertising, service contracts, and philanthropy. Chapters were established in ten major cities. Operating on the basic presupposition that "the earth is the Lord's, and the fulness thereof,"[24] the Breadbasket strategy is as follows:

1. *Investigation*–A target company is researched with respect to its total business posture, and then visited by a committee of clergymen. Data is requested of the president. The data includes items such as the latest report to the Economic Opportunity Commission, a complete breakdown of all jobs according to race, and a listing of all concerns with which the company does business. If the company refuses to release the information, that is sufficient grounds for a withdrawal of patronage. If the information is given, the second step is taken.

2. *Education*–This is self-education. The chapter familiarizes its constituency with the facts and draws up a set of demands to be presented to the target company.

3. *Negotiation*–Demands are formally presented and a time period given for compliance. If good faith is evidenced within the designated time period, a covenant is agreed upon and signed by the principals, signaling a new relationship of respect and justice. If good faith is not demonstrated, the chapter moves to the fourth step.

4. *Demonstration*–While demonstration may include picketing and leafleting, it involves primarily the use of pulpits, public media, and word of mouth announcements to inform blacks and other persons of goodwill that the target company has been declared off limits. As a rule, it is just a short while before the company feels the pinch and the loss of its "good" name, and thereupon agrees to the demands.

5. *Reconciliation*–The company and the community are reconciled. A covenant is signed, and blacks are informed that it is now all right to patronize the company.

The Breadbasket strategy is a workable one. It is rational, responsible, and redemptive. However, there is one major drawback. Economic injustice is so widespread, and those equipped to carry on the struggle are so few in number, that it is difficult to implement the strategy on a wide scale. There have been instances where companies other than the one in immediate question invited Operation Breadbasket to look them over and set their house in order. It should be noted that Breadbasket does not concern itself with recruitment and training, which are viewed as company responsibilities. Operation Push, a split from Operation Bread-basket, employs a strategy identical to that of Breadbasket. Both stress the need for blacks to support black business wherever possible, and both have sponsored black business expositions to raise the visibility level of black businesses.

The Greater New York chapter of Operation Breadbasket ran up a string of successive victories over Taystee Bread, Wonder Bread, Drake's Bakeries, Mays Department Stores, Abraham & Straus, Martins Department Stores, Coca Cola Bottling Company of New York, Canada Dry, Robert Hall, Sealtest Foods, and Pepsi Cola Bottling Company. In most instances, it was not necessary to call for a boycott. The mere threat of such an action caused company officials to accede to the demands.

The most formidable foe ever faced by the Greater New York chapter was the Great Atlantic and Pacific Tea Company, a company with sales in excess of 50 billion dollars per annum, and a net profit (after taxes) of less than 1 percent. After several unsuccessful attempts to meet with William Kane, president of A & P, the chapter's ministerial leaders decided on a course of direct action. Twenty-two clergymen gathered in Grand Central Station on the morning of January 27, 1971, and proceeded from there to the executive suite of A & P. A knock on the door resulted in its being opened, whereupon the preachers moved in and began an occupation of the offices, which lasted some thirty-six hours, culminating in arrests for criminal trespassing. The widespread publicity resulting from this action alerted the general public to the unjust dealings of A & P with the black community. The company's products were declared off limits to black appetites. Many whites joined in the struggle. Other mass arrests followed, including those of the Reverend Jesse Jackson and the Reverend Ralph Abernathy, president of Southern Christian Leadership Conference. As a result of such activities, a ground swell of support developed in the New York City area, extending even to Rochester, New York. Thirty-three major organizations gave the campaign unreserved endorsement. These included the United Farm Workers of America, the Congress of African Peoples, the National Council of Churches, the Catholic Senate of Manhattan, the Episcopal Diocese of Brooklyn and Long Island, the Catholic Senate of Brooklyn and Long Island, the Baptist Ministers Conference of New York and Vicinity, the Commission on Interfaith Activities of the Union of American Hebrew Congregations, the North Jersey Federation of Reformed Synagogues, the Harlem Ministers' Interfaith Association, the New York Inter-religious Clergy Coalition, the Brooklyn Catholic Inter-racial Council, the Long Island Council of Churches, the New Rochelle Council of Churches, the Council of Churches of the City of New York, the National Disciples of Christ, the Council of Black Elected Officials, the National Welfare Rights Organization, the Vulcan Society (black firemen), the New York Urban League, Block Associations, and numerous other groups. Huntington Hartford, grandson of the founder and a major shareholder in A & P, gave his endorsement and called a press conference to publicly declare his support.

The impact was significant. A & P sales were dealt a severe blow. The value of company stock steadily fell. When the action began, A & P stock was selling at $34.00 per share. It has not risen above $8.00 in the past three years.

William Kane, the president who refused to meet with the ministers, and whose action brought about the boycott, was kicked upstairs to the position of chairman.

99

This was either a case of elimination by elevation or a reward for recalcitrance. William Longacre was elected president and appeared more reasonable and seemed anxious to come to terms. Several meetings were held with him in a Manhattan hotel. It was obvious that he was not his own man; a ventriloquist was behind the scenes. He agreed to sign a covenant, but one drafted by the company with more shadow than substance, which was totally unacceptable.

The momentum generated by the mass arrests and the many endorsements picked up speed. Jackson and Abernathy scheduled press conferences and called for a national boycott. It appeared to the New York chapter that, for the first time in American history, blacks were about to move collectively on a nationwide scale in the interest of economic justice. That hope was short-lived. Nothing was done at the national level to implement the announced action. Greater New York was the only area of regular activity. The chapter could have settled for a covenant which covered A & P operations in the New York area, but this was unacceptable since the originally stated goal was that of a national covenant covering all A & P operations and installations. It should be acknowledged that significant changes have taken place in A & P's behavior in the New York community. The percentage of blacks has increased at all levels. Several black companies have entered into a contractual relationship with the company. The boycott has not been lifted. Hence, many persons still refuse to patronize A & P. It should also be noted that for the first time in two years, the company realized a profit in the first quarter of 1974.

The lessons learned to date from the A & P encounter are crucial to the development of any program of economic justice. First, blacks can effectively organize at the local level to challenge economic injustice. Second, the more obstinate the adversary, the greater the degree of public support. Third, it requires no more energy to fight a large company than it does to fight a smaller one. Fourth, it is not difficult, when the issues are clear and properly presented, to galvanize diverse religious and civic groups into an effective coalition.

Blacks in America have never moved in concert against any major business concern. Such an effort would serve well to inform and heighten the collective conscience of blacks concerning their tremendous but latent consumption power. Economic equity spells power. Equity is owed to blacks, but there is no disposition on the part of powerful economic pharaohs to grant it; it must be seized by means of creative coercion.

The third component in an effective program of creative coercion is that of the politicization of black numerical strength. Ghetto dwellers have few representatives in government to plead their case. The gap between numerical strength and political power is greater than, though not as devastating as, the economic gap between blacks and whites. At the national level, blacks hold less than 4 percent of the congressional seats, and 0 percent of the senatorial seats. This is the picture at that level where primary decisions are made with respect to "Life, Liberty, and the Pursuit of Happiness."

The problem of low representation is due in major measure to the long period of disenfranchisement, brought to an end less than ten years ago with passage of the Voting Rights Bill of 1965. But in the North, where political action was an easier enterprise, blacks demonstrated great apathy, mainly because of a basic distrust of the political system. Politics as a means of liberation is, at best, highly suspect in the eyes of the blacks. It is a game of nonchoice, where no real differences can be detected in the two major parties. Furthermore, blacks see little that politicians have done to ease their condition, not to mention the deliverance from that condition. It may be that blacks who are politically disinterested, through some sixth sense, see politics as nonredemptive. If that is the case, they are correct, for "politics is means, not Messiah."[25] However, this does not negate the importance of the "means." Politics is not inherently uncaring. There are politicians who do not care. The surge for power on the part of blacks has profound political implications for their general well-being. To dismiss or ignore this reality is to court cultural disaster. As evidenced by the election of blacks in increasingly large numbers throughout the South, black political leadership that is sensitive to human needs can and does make a difference. Through a process of critical examination and selection, black communities the nation over can insure the production of a new breed of politicians, men and women who view themselves as protagonists for the poor, and interpret their mission as that of dealing with the greedy in order to heal the needy.

Important to the idea of a revolutionary confrontation with the system is the principle of coalition. Although blacks are primarily concerned with the problems related to their ghetto existence, the reality of the class problem in America must be acknowledged. A commonality of affliction due to poverty affects many groups. Demonic structures are not only racist; they are also political and economic. If racism ceased to exist (and there is no indication that it will), the class problem would still persist. The economic well-being of the majority of Americans is very tenuous. Lundberg says at the outset of his book:

Most Americans—citizens of the wealthiest, most power-ful and most ideal-swathed country in the world—by a very wide margin own nothing more than their household goods, a few glittering gadgets such as automobiles and television sets (usually purchased on the installment plan, many at second hand) and the clothes on their backs. A horde if not a majority of Americans live in shacks, cabins, hovels, shanties, hand-me-down Victorian eyesores, rickety tenements and flaky apartment buildings.[26]

The vast majority of the nation's people live either in poverty or on the cutting edge of poverty. The average worker cannot afford an illness of a few months' duration. If such is the plight of the working class, how harrowing must be the lot of the unemployed. The September 1978 figures from the U. S. Department of Labor's Bureau of Labor Statistics reveal the following:

Unemployed Whites	16 and over	5.2%
Unemployed Blacks & others	16 and over	11.8%
Unemployed Males/White	20 and over	3.1%
Unemployed Males/Black	20 and over	7.1%
Unemployed Females/White	20 and over	5.7%
Unemployed Females/Black	20 and over	10.8%
Unemployed Teenagers/White	16 to 19	12.8%
Unemployed Teenagers/Black male	16 to 19	34.0%
Unemployed Teenagers/White female	16 to 19	15.9%
Unemployed Teenagers/Black female	16 to 19	39.7%

While the percentage of unemployed blacks is twice the number of unemployed whites, the total number of unemployed whites exceeds the number of unemployed blacks. Their common tribulation is in itself sufficient reason for forming an alliance for joint action. If the working class of people (black and white) recognized their marginal existence at the mercy of the ruling class, they would unite to deal with their common enemy. They would also recognize their affinity with the unemployed and seek the formation of a coalition to work for an equitable distribution of the nation's wealth.

It is abundantly clear that blacks are affected by the problem of color *and* class, while most whites are affected by the problem of class. Color is the chief obstacle to coalescence. The racist ethos has created for whites an illusory notion concerning their place under the sun. This is the primary problem standing in the way of coalition. So long-standing and widespread is the reality of racism that blacks are naturally suspicious of attempts to form black and white alliances. Well-meaning whites who truly desire justice for all will have to guard against all appearances of that brand of liberalism which is marked by a spirit of paternalism. Blacks would rather "hoe their own row" than relate to whites on anything less than a peer basis.

In this writer's view, the most logical arena for attempts at coalition is the religious community. The ecumenism demonstrated in the previously mentioned A & P confrontation is a strong indicator of the existing possibilities. In that situation, white churchmen entered the fray with a clear recognition and acceptance of the established black leadership. Coalition can be effective, but only when respect is real and when the achievement of justice is recognized as the prelude to reconciliation. At any rate, the liberation of blacks remains essentially a black concern.

What instrumentality is available to blacks for confronting the system and dealing with demonic structures? There is but one, that unique religio-social institution called the black church. The Church, wherever it exists, is inherently social. In local terms, the Church is a society of sinners hammering out its redemption under the auspices of grace. The Church is social by definition. Why then is it necessary to speak of the black church as a religio-social institution? If Christianity is concerned about man in the totality of his relationships, why is such a characterization important? This tag of identification is used because of essential differences between the black church and the white church. Because of its origin, affliction, worship, witness, and mission, it has had to be more social then any other religious institution on American soil. A deep social consciousness was forced upon it by cultural conditions and circumstances.

Certain African antecedents made the process simpler and easier. Though apparently stripped of their African heritage, there remained in and with the slaves at least one ethical carry-over: the idea of the "together community." Basic to the African way of life is a view of society in terms of mutual obligation, as opposed to the Western emphasis on individual rights. The statement "the wolf is in the pack and the pack is in the wolf" is applicable to the African situation. William Conton expresses well the African spirit:

> And then my father went on to remind me that I had started to climb a palm tree that was high and difficult to climb. That many were watching my progress, and much fruit awaited me on the successful conclusion of my climb. But then he went on to warn me that if I failed to reach the top, those both living and dead would curse me for having failed them. And if I reached the top simply to gorge myself with fruit, I would surely become sick and fall to the ground and die. But if I reached the top and returned to my people, to share with them the fruits of my labor, then all would honor and praise me and thank those who had brought me to life.[27]

No doctrine of rugged individualism has ever gotten off the ground in Africa. The sanctity of individual personality is inseparably tied to the sanctity of the group; and since all of life is fundamentally religious, religion is social and the social is religious.

105

These humans from Africa were brought to the New World with their souls (the essence of being) intact. Tribal units were broken up; families were disjointed; and persons from different tribes, speaking different languages, were thrown together to make easier the new socialization process. But with their souls intact, there remained an innate capacity for receiving the revelation of God in Jesus Christ. These motley groupings, strangers to one another, learned a new language, developed a new dialect, put it together in God's name, and became one of God's new creations: the black church. They were bound together by four distinctives: blood, blackness, bondage, and the new birth. The black church was for the slaves, and to this day remains the American counterpart of the African extended family. It more closely resembles the Christian communities of the New Testament than any other church in the Western world. *Koinonia* does not have to be designed and promoted. It derives quite naturally from the factors already cited. DuBois wrote eighty years ago:

> As a social group the Negro Church may be said to have antedated the Negro family on American soil; as such it has preserved, on the one hand, many functions of tribal organization, and on the other hand, many of the family functions. Its tribal functions are shown in its religious activity, its social authority, and general guiding and coordinating work; its family functions are shown by the fact that the church is a center of social life and intercourse, acts as newspaper and intelligence bureau, is the center of amusements—indeed, is the world in which the Negro moves and acts. So far-reaching are these functions of the church that its organization is almost political.[28]

The development of a social gospel theology was not necessary for blacks. James Cone's *Black Theology and*

Black Power is mainly the restatement of positions that once flowered and almost died. It is a case of old wine having been put in new bottles. The religious and the social have been one for blacks. Worship is a collective experience of the living Word. Singing is a union of body and soul in wondrous ecstasy. Preaching is antiphonal. One hour is not adequate for the public worship of God. When one experiences eternity, the clock has little significance. Persons touch each other before, during, and after the service proper. The African concept of community remains central. The emphasis is on "we" instead of "me." One's "me-ness" is authenticated only as it contributes to and participates in a glorious "we-ness" under God.

In the Lord's service, the Kingdom comes on earth through a corporate, communal emphasis and experience. Karl Barth, in his *Church Dogmatics,* points out four levels of humanity on an ascending scale:

1) "Eye to eye" relationship (seeing one another).

2) Mutual speech and hearing (communicating: talking to and hearing one another).

3) Mutual assistance (helping one another; sharing).

4) All of the other three levels together with a spirit of joy *(koinonia* and *agape).* [29]

The black church is the most visible expression of this kind of humanity on the American scene.

The black church became the new Africa. It was "the extended family" restored, under the leadership of Jesus Christ, the great High Priest, and under the earthly direction of the black preacher who was prophet, priest, and village chief. Conceived in the womb of social crises

107

and born as a result of the disparity between Christian faith and social policy, it has been inseparably related from the beginning to the black *sitz im Leben* (situation in life) to the sufferings and deprivations of an oppressed people. It has provided a sense of belonging and filled the need for approval. Since its inception it has been the largest and most significant of all racial enterprises. By and large, the social advances of the race have had their origins in the black church: the struggle for human rights, battles for economic equity, efforts for fair and decent housing, and warfare against the racist ethos.

The black church has been and still remains the connecting rod between black history and black hope. It is the only institution on the island that has historic continuity. It is the largest base of numerical strength. It is the one place where the vision of a nobler life is lifted up regularly. It views life as perennial struggle by people in pilgrimage. And because of its nondependence on the larger society, it is free to be prophetic. When compared with the white church in America, sharp differences are readily observable:

Black Church	White Church
church of the oppressed	church of the oppressors
theology of survival	theology of success
theology of immanence	theology of transcendence
prophetic	priestly
free pulpit	restricted pulpit
spontaneity in worship	rigidity in worship
social ferment	status quo oriented
activistic affliction	apathy
substance	shadow
heterogeneous	homogeneous

108

While the aforementioned differentiations do not apply absolutely to the black church and the white church, the preponderance of evidence weighs heavily in favor of such a typology. Racism has rendered the white church spiritually powerless. Many black churches also have failed to exercise the prophetic function. Judgment is upon them for failure to act in terms of their freedom, a freedom that is inherently present in any community of believers that is not bound to the culture in which it finds itself. Black preachers, in particular, enjoy a status unlike that of all other clergymen. They are answerable, in the main, only to the God they serve. They need not ask permission to be prophetic. They and the churches they lead are the logical leaders in the encounter with systemic sin and entrenched evil.

The black preacher, unfortunately, is often a hindrance to the advancement of the black cause. Some are inactive in the struggle because of their failure to see the social implications of the Gospel. They are unconscious allies of racistic religion. It is not uncommon to hear a black clergyman say: "My task is to preach the Gospel and win souls to Jesus Christ. Social betterment will come only through the salvation of men." Such a theological stance not only makes for ministerial apathy; it also can serve to render an entire congregation socially impotent.

To awaken many black preachers to the prophetic task is an awesome but necessary responsibility. This difficulty was painfully dramatized at the beginning of the A & P struggle in New York City. While the Breadbasket clergymen were occupying the A & P executive offices, a black ministerial conference was in session. It was decided that those attending the conference should be alerted and enlisted in the effort. The following letter was written:

GOD IN THE GHETTO

My Brethren,

I'm sure you know by now that I along with 21 others of our ministerial brethren have occupied the Executive Offices of A & P at 420 Lexington Avenue since 9:30 A.M. yesterday. We are here in the interest of justice for our people. Since coming here to declare the truth and righteousness demanded of God, we have discovered that the A & P situation is worse than we had ever imagined. Nearly 500 people work here under the leadership of President William Kane. Only a handful are Black. Of 137 top executives working here, only *one* is Black. There are no Blacks at all in the Accounting Department. A & P operates out of a plantation ethic and has no intention of dealing justly with our people.

Brethren, we are here. We are tired and hungry, but absolutely determined. I appeal to you now for your active support. We need your presence here today. We cannot telephone out. A & P officials are attempting to keep the Press out. I pray that you will find it possible to leave the Conference around 2:30 or 3:00 and come here as a body in the name of Jesus Christ to press the just demands of our people who have been historically victimized by the economic evils of a wicked social system. You and I are comfortably situated. We are a privileged group. But for millions of our brothers and sisters, hunger pains dart through their bodies. We have to be here not for our sake, but for the future's sake. I am here because Jesus couldn't make it. If He were in town, I'm convinced that He would be here with us. I ask of you your prayers and your presence.

For the Brethren,

William A. Jones, Jr.

To the surprise of the Breadbasket clergymen and to the shame of the ministerial conference, only one preacher responded in a positive manner.

In order for the latent power of the black church to become manifest, it is essential that a wholistic understanding of the Christian Gospel be at the top of the agenda for black theological education. The black preacher is easily the freest man in the American pulpit, but freedom devoid of understanding serves only to perpetuate black powerlessness. By virtue of its calling, its strengths, its continuity, its freedom, and the power inherent in that freedom, the black church can readily become "reservation headquarters." The capability is present. Only the will "to be" is needed.

The collective power of members of individual congregations has been demonstrated over and over again. They have erected new edifices, established credit unions, built low-income housing, and served as rallying bases for movements in behalf of social justice. The great need is for the "people power" already evidenced at the congregational level to be extended to areas of community enterprise. Many local congregations are sufficiently strong to sponsor community-based institutions and enterprises that will lead to economic self-sufficiency within the ghetto. If and when the power of all black churches is collectivized for a national thrust, the day of total liberation will be clearly in view.

Better than thirty years ago, Richard Wright wrote,

> Our churches are where we dip our tired bodies in cool springs of hope, where we retain our wholeness and humanity, despite the blows of death from the Bosses.[30]

The "blows of death" continue to come. The "bosses" of the system must be confronted with the demands of the Creator. The autocracy of pleasure must be replaced by the democratization of pleasure and pain.

If the struggle ends with the oppressor and the oppressed living in a climate of reconciliation, let God be praised. If not, let God still be praised. For He has placed

Himself on the side of the victimized masses; and through their conquests in His name, the Kingdom will come on earth as it is in Heaven.

FOOTNOTES

1. Charles P. Hamilton, Jr., *The Nixon Theology*, p. 38.

2. Ferdinand Lundberg, *The Rich and the Super-Rich*, p. 13.

3. Ibid., p. 297.

4. Ibid., p. 358.

5. Wright Mills, *The Power Elite*, p. 290.

6. *Congressional Record*, April 4, 1967, p. S4582.

7. Aristotle, "Politics," *The Works of Aristotle*, vol. 11, *The Great Books of the Western World*, ed. Robert M. Hutchins, 9:503.

8. Arnold Schuchter, *Reparations*, p. 69.

9. The Declaration of Independence.

10. Colin Morris, *Unyoung–Uncolored–Unpoor*, p. 82.

11. Emil Brunner, as quoted in ibid., p. 94.

12. Ted R. Gurr, as quoted in Schuchter, p. 32.

13. Jose M. Bonino, "Christians and the Political Revolution," *The Development Apocalypse*, ed. Stephen C. Rose, p. 108.

14. Jacques Ellul, *Violence*, p. 167.

15. Isaiah 40:4-5.

16. Stokley Carmichael, "What We Want," *The Boston Sunday Herald*, October 2, 1966.

17. Samuel F. Yette, *The Choice: The Issue of Black Survival in America*, p. 18.

18. Dan. 3:18.

19. Dan. 1:8.

20. Acts 5:29.

21. I Thess. 5:22.

22. Daniel Thompson, *The Negro Leadership Class,* pp. 58-79.

23. Charles H. Wesley, *Richard Allen–Apostle of Freedom,* pp. 239-40.

24. Psalm 24:1.

25. Will D. Campbell and James J. Holloway, *Up to Our Steeples in Politics,* p. 71.

26. Lundberg, p. 1.

27. William Conton, from The African Writers Series, not copyrighted.

28. W. E. Burghardt DuBois, *The Philadelphia Negro,* p. 201.

29. Karl Barth, *Church Dogmatics,* ed. T. F. Torrance and G. W. Bromley, vol. 3, pt. 11, p. 250.

30. Richard Wright, in "12 Million Black Voices."

8

Summary and Conclusion

THE GHETTO is the most visible and the most profound symbol of the American System, that systematic, sociocultural design which created and perpetuates the existence of two cultures, one white and one black under one flag. Its visibility level is so high that it stands out as the most serious indictment of the democratic ethic. But worse than this is the existence of the ghetto phenomenon in "a Bible land and God-fearing country." This is the primary contradiction alive and at work in the body politic. The social aberrations resulting from a racist ethos buttressed and inspired by racistic religion, represent concretely the very antithesis of the Gospel's view of the "abundant life." The ghetto is a pot of desolation and death where futility abounds and where economic genocide is a current reality.

Throughout the length of the black experience in America, one basic, burning query has sounded forth: How does one deal with a racist order? How does one change a social system that is not simply sick, but deeply demonic? What method does one employ to overcome a

114

system whose holy trinity is capitalism, racism, and militarism? The depth of the problem is made greater by the white church's involvement, both initially and continually, in the diatribe. The church sanctioned slavery, supported segregation, and continues to give assent to inequity by its acquiescent posture. Blacks have surveyed the national landscape and concluded that white America has no desire to rectify long-standing injustice. Repentance is rare, and reparation is nowhere on the agenda. The white church has capitulated to culture and serves as the soothing conscience rather than the critical conscience of the state. Little help is available from that quarter. Only a few saints can be located "in Caesar's household." The pain predicament of Black people has become more aggravated by the presence of a "born again" believer in the White House. President Jimmy Carter would have remained a "peanut farmer" had not Blacks en masse cast their ballots for him. He, to date, has shown a basic insensitivity to the cries of the masses. His former membership in the Trilateral Conference, coupled with his strong support of existing economic arrangements has caused him to be called in some quarters a "Rockefeller Republican." His appointment of Andrew Young as United Nations Ambassador is regarded as a sop thrown to Blacks, i.e., position without power and symbol devoid of substance. His emphasis on human rights has been selective rather than universal. Mr. Carter's "born again" status appealed greatly to the deep spiritual sensitivity of Blacks. Black preachers across America urged their congregants to vote for the man who was unashamed to own his Lord. But now, due to Mr. Carter's own inaction, questions long overdue are being raised: "What does he mean when he declares, 'I've been born again'? What is the ethical content of his faith? Do we, in the next Presidential election, look to another?"

Given the poignancy of the Black condition, the answer to the latter query may very well be a resounding "Yes!"

The Black response with respect to methodology has been threefold: (1) A small minority believes that the answer resides in an ethic of black separatism; (2) an even smaller minority espouses an ethic of violent revolution; (3) the majority leans toward an ethic of creative coercion, where existing power is seriously utilized to democratize both pleasure and pain in the land.

The most viable instrumentality in the nation to give leadership in this necessary struggle is the black church, numerically strong, and the only institution on the "island" with historic continuity. Its affinity with the religion of Jesus Christ is the clearest and most discernible in American culture. It lives closer to Calvary than its white counterpart, and is therefore in a better position to spend itself in encounter and confrontation for the redemption and liberation of the captives. The black church's social mission is twofold: (1) that of dealing with the victimizers in terms of judgment and demands for justice, and (2) that of healing the victims, torn and riveted by the evils of the system.

Recognizing that all men deserve "a right to the tree of life," the black church, when properly performing its prophetic functions, will seek reconciliation between the oppressors and the oppressed, but only on terms of equity and justice. Any other arrangement is a facsimile of the present arrangement. The collective conscience of the darker races of the world steadily grows and expands. The warning is out: "We will no longer be the starving victims of those who steal." The New Testament supports those who contend that equality of scarcity is preferable to inequality of abundance. The basic issue is none other than life itself. For that fundamental reason, a luta continua (the struggle continues).

Part II

SERMONS

1

Back-door Divinity

And she brought forth her firstborn son, and wrapped him in swaddling clothes, and laid him in a manger; because there was no room for them in the inn (Lk. 2:7).

He didn't have to do it, but He did. Christ Jesus, "being in the form of God, thought it not robbery to be equal with God: but made himself of no reputation, and took upon him the form of a servant, and was made in the likeness of men" (Phil. 2:6, 7). He didn't have to do it, but He did. "The Word became flesh and dwelt among us" (Jn. 1:14, NASB). God became man. The Sovereign elected to become a servant. The Eternal showed up in time and space. He didn't have to do it, but He did. For Him to simply come our way would be enough, one would think. Just to visit this planet and give mortals a glimpse of God should be sufficient, one would think. To

119

simply let us know that the Lord God Almighty was not detached nor disinterested would suffice, one would think.

But, quite to the contrary, in His mind that alone was not enough. More than a passing view of Himself was necessary. Something other than a sudden entry and a quick exit was needed. The strategy called for a sojourn, a tabernacling, a flesh-and-blood involvement, not for a little while and not for a long, long time, but for thirty and three years, long enough to move from helpless infancy to mature manhood, and long enough to make an indelible imprint on humankind as to who and what God really is.

That He came in flesh is enough to warm youthful hearts, encourage mature spirits, and send the elderly to their graves in peace. That He elected to clothe Himself in our mortality ought to be enough to turn every eye and every heart Godward, but He went far beyond incarnation or enfleshment. He did more, much more, than remove His royal robe and replace it with the garb of our humanity. He came our way by way of the back door. The God who created all that is—Heaven and earth; sky and sea; sun, moon, and stars; every living thing there is—the God who is omnipotent, omniscient, omnipresent divinity, came to see us through a back door.

While certain Greeks were delving in philosophy, and while certain Romans were trying to conquer the world, and while certain Jews were corrupting religion, God was on His way to a stable in Bethlehem. His arrival, His appearing, however you view it or measure it, was purely and plainly a back-door entry. In terms of place—Nazareth and Bethlehem. In terms of time—when not expected. In terms of people—Joseph and Mary. In terms of environment—a little barn, some swaddling clothes, and an ox crib. I cannot help describing Him as back-door divinity, and I do it with righteous respect and reverence. He didn't have to do it, but He did.

Of course, that's the appraisal from where we sit, with our limited vision and finite understanding. The faithful, out of gratitude, declare, "He didn't have to do it, but He did." That, in a real sense, is our canticle of praise. That's the way all recipients of grace must talk. To be the beneficiary of a love not deserved and of favor not earned calls forth perpetual gratitude. When I consider His marvelous grace, I have to tell Him, "God, You didn't have to do it, but You did."

But from His perspective of totality, where "from everlasting to everlasting" He is, I get the impression that He declares, "I had to do it, and I did." "With me," says God, "I came to the world by way of the back door by both choice and constraint. I willed it that way. And My will involves no contradiction between desire and determination. I wanted to and I had to. I wanted to because I had to, and I had to because I wanted to. I willed it that way. My back-door arrival was consonant with My will."

"All right, Lord. Who am I and who are we to argue with You? That aspect of Your arrival is final. The case is closed. You wanted to because You had to, and You had to because You wanted to. Thank You, Lord. But now, Lord, let me look at the happening from where I sit. Let me use this capacity to think and to reason You've given me to ponder and reflect on Your back-door arrival."

I hear Him say, "Go right ahead. That's one reason I gave it to you."

Back-door divinity! Yes! That's what He was when He came our way. But why? With all the front doors available, why a back-door entry? That's the approach of a thief in the night. Why would He come via the back door? Why Nazareth and Bethlehem when there were Athens, Rome, and Jerusalem? Why Joseph and Mary when people of prominence dwelt in every chief city? Why a barn, swaddling clothes, and an ox crib when creature comforts were available? Why this back-door entrance to the place of our abode? We feel our way through the darkness of the Bethlehem night, and as we move toward the manger, He gives us light. We seek, and in seeking we find.

He came by way of the back door to avoid and to assault the arrogance of power. A little of it seems to whet the appetite for more and more and even more. I have seen it at every level of life. It is conspicuous in corporate board-rooms, at command levels in the military, in the halls of academia, in the chambers of government, and among the so-called princes of the Church. This craving for power is also present at lower levels. I've witnessed it in factory foremen, supervisors in offices, people in all kinds of uniforms, churchmen with various and sundry titles, and even in receptionists anxious to show their authority.

Power is an awesome and awful allurement. Lord Acton wisely said, "Power tends to corrupt and absolute power tends to corrupt absolutely." A man wiser than he has written, "Let him who thinks he stands take heed lest he fall" (I Cor. 10:12, NASB).

The ultimate absurdity of power is that they who possess it have a tendency to try and play God. Raw and raucous was the prevailing power when God came via the back door, with Athens the acme of thought power, Rome the apogee of military and political power, and Jerusalem the citadel of religious power, and each one of them perverted to the core! In coming through the back door, He avoided them and thereby assaulted them. He refused to let evil even mildly participate in His plan. By avoiding these perverted centers of power, He shook them from center to circumference. Herod trembled,

Jerusalem shook, Rome quaked, and a signal was sent all the way to Athens that she too was under judgment. And ever since, the word has been out that the wicked shall not stand. For "the kingdom of this world has become the kingdom of our Lord, and of His Christ" (Rev. 11:15, NASB), and "of his kingdom there shall be no end" (Lk. 1:33). The Almighty, He who is all-power, came by way of the back door to avoid and thereby assault the arrogance of power.

He came that way for another reason. That was the only door that would bid Him "welcome." A soul in beggar's apparel, although a King, would elicit no warm response at the front door of sinful humanity. Herod, you remember, was a member of the front-door crowd; and as soon as he heard of His arrival, he sought to kill Him. How vivid is my own memory of the absence of front-door hospitality in this land, that shameful period when certain of us, on account of color, were considered fit only for back-door entry. As a sociology student, I read of a black man in Mississippi who owned certain properties which he rented to whites; but in order to collect his rent, he had to go to the back door. In those places where caste and class reigned supreme, even poor whites had to suffer back-door status. Whenever and wherever one's personhood is ignored or demeaned, the front-door—back-door syndrome is alive and active.

It is interesting that those who are relegated to back-door status are in most instances the ones who work inside the back door—cooks, maids, janitors, service people—errand boys and the like. And these, in the main, are people who are given to warmth and hospitality. In the days when hobos were common in America, they'd get something to eat, not by knocking on front doors of nice homes, but by going to the back door and beseeching servants to feed them. At the back door they'd get sympathy, empathy, consideration, and compassion. They weren't welcome at the front door. Say what you will, those who are powerless and weak are, on the whole, more given to a hospitable spirit than those who are powerful and wicked. God knew that Joseph and Mary wouldn't be received by that innkeeper. They weren't welcome at the front door; but, out back, a barn was anxious to receive them. That was the only door that would bid Him welcome.

Lastly, He came by way of the back door because that's the location of most of His children. It is not my purpose to deal with the thorny issue of social disparity. My main concern is to lift up the truth about God's concern for the whole of humanity, and the unalterable, undeniable reality is that most of His children are back-door dwellers. I have touched down on every continent under heaven. I've felt the bitter winds of the Arctic, the chill of a Russian winter, and the warm zephyrs of West Africa. I've sailed Victoria Harbor in the Crown Colony of Hong Kong, and I've gone by steamer along the Rhine through the lush vineyards of West Germany. I've walked the streets of London and viewed the white cliffs of Dover. I've seen South America and rested beneath the Caribbean sky. I've been caught in the rush hour in both Tokyo and Barcelona, and I've traversed some of the great open spaces in Australia. I've traveled America from top to bottom and from coast to coast. And everywhere, throughout my Father's world, most of His children are back-door dwellers. Many are hungry and dying of malnutrition. Many are crying for a taste of freedom. Some are living fairly well, but struggling to hold on to what they have. And all of them sing the lament, "I'm rolling thru an unfriendly world."

But God told me to tell you that He's back-door divinity. He came to befriend the friendless. He came to cheer the cheerless. He came to save the lost. He came to give light to our darkness. He came to puncture pride. He came to assault arrogance. He came our way that we might have life.

Don't you hear Him speaking, "The Spirit of the Lord is upon me, because he hath anointed me to preach the gospel to the poor; he hath sent me to heal the brokenhearted; to preach deliverance to the captives, and recovering of sight to the blind, to set at liberty them that are bruised, to preach the acceptable year of the Lord" (Lk. 4:18, 19). That's what He said and that's what He did—from Bethlehem to Jerusalem, from the back door to the front door.

And now He speaks from Heaven, saying, "Behold, I stand at the door, and knock; if any man hear my voice, and open the door, I will come in to him, and will sup with him, and he with me" (Rev. 3:20). He's knocking at all doors now. For "all have gone astray" (Isa. 53:6). In God's eye, all of us are back-door dwellers. And if you open up and let Him come in, He'll give you eternal salvation, peace that flows like a river, joy everlasting, a song to sing, and a story to tell.

Blessed assurance, Jesus is mine!
Oh, what a foretaste of glory divine!
Heir of salvation, purchase of God,
Born of His Spirit, washed in His blood.

This is my story, this is my song,
Praising my Saviour, all the day long,
This is my story, this is my song,
Praising my Saviour all the day long.

Fanny J. Crosby

125

"Lord, thank You for coming by the back-door route. From where You sit, You had to do it. But from where I sit—a back-door dweller saved by grace—You didn't have to do it, but You did. And I'm glad, so glad, You did."

2

In Flesh for Flesh

*And the Word was made flesh, and dwelt among us,
(and we beheld his glory, the glory as of the only begotten of
the Father,) full of grace and truth (Jn. 1:14).*

The Christian faith is often charged with being esoteric
and ethereal, a religion so heavenly minded that it's no
earthly good. Certain critics, historically and presently,
have looked on Christians and accused them of espous-
ing an ethic that is tragically divorced from the problems
and pains of this world, and the charge is not without
some basis in fact.

Many who claim an allegiance to Jesus Christ make no
quarrel with the charge. They live under the conviction
that God is not concerned about this world. They view
"the world, the flesh, and the devil" as the unholy trinity,
fully operative on the planet earth. For them, the material world is a house of horrors, the locus of inevitable

evil, the devil's province and playground. Such a view eventuates in detachment and isolation from the world's struggles. It often leads to various forms of asceticism. In a real sense, it hands the world over carte blanche to the emissaries of evil.

That's terrible enough, but something more deeply disturbing takes place. If we ascribe ineluctable evil to the material world, we who claim Christ as Lord of all do violence to His incarnation. We devalue the divine entry. We belittle the birth in Bethlehem. We throw a smoke screen over His earthly ministry. That, precisely, is our perennial problem, and it almost always stems from the notion that the material world is inherently evil. So deeply entrenched in history is this attitude that early in the life of the Church there developed a doctrine called docetism, a doctrine which held that the eternal Christ did not actually become flesh but merely seemed to be a man. Jesus Christ, said the docetists, was an apparition; the incarnation was an illusion. Since matter is evil, God could not possibly appear in human flesh. The Church Fathers wisely declared this view heretical, but across the centuries, and even now, the heresy persists, existentially if not essentially.

Of course, nobody seriously questions the reality of the Jesus of history anymore. All of the world's major religions accept the fact that there did live a man named Jesus. Christians everywhere declare without wavering that in "the fullness of the time" (Gal. 4:4), beneath the black bosom of a Palestinian sky, while a city slumbered in the hush of night, God came to see us! In a dirty barn in Bethlehem, on a rocky road between Hebron and Jerusalem, "the Word became flesh." He who is the "Ancient of days" (Dan. 7:9), previously hidden from human eyes—remote spirit, detached divinity, unseen reality, the God of the ages, the one true God—divested Himself of some of His prerogatives, removed His royal robe, uncrowned His holy head, departed His throne, forsook the songs of seraphim and the chants of cherubim, and entered our mortality.

"The Word became flesh, and dwelt among us" (Jn. 1:14). The Immortal became mortal. The God who was way off yonder came as close as breathing. God exposed Himself to evil and enigma, to "the slings and arrows of outrageous fortune." How far He came! How low He stooped! From Heaven to earth, from divinity to dust, from royalty to rejection. What condescension! And yet, it was as much ascent as descent. Jesus is not simply Karl Barth's "wholly other, breaking in perpendicularly from above." Though He came from the top down, He also came from the bottom up. He broke in on our pilgrimage from beneath. He came as "a root out of a dry ground" (Isa. 53:2), up through forty and two generations. Eternal goodness came as a child.

How human is our Lord—God with us, God among us—in back alleys and on public squares. Seeking no favors, asking for no privilege, giving no sanction to caste and class, "the Word became flesh, and dwelt among us." Christians accept His incarnation hardly without a question. It is the implications of His incarnation that pose a problem for many people. The real problem is not His coming "in flesh," but His coming "for flesh." It's not the divine method that disturbs some; it's the divine motivation. The true testimony is that "God sent not his Son into the world to condemn the world; but that the world through him might be saved" (Jn. 3:17). That's total liberation.

God loves the world. He has never given up on the world which He made. If He had, He long ago would have stopped the procreation process. He has promised to make all things new. His plan is that of a redeemed materialism, the release of the whole creation from its bondage. Jesus came in flesh, for flesh. If you don't understand this, yours is a low view of the incarnation; and you cannot help remembering Calvary while forgetting Bethlehem. Jesus lived with us before He died for us. Calvary was the climax of the incarnation. Calvary was the natural conclusion of coming in flesh, for flesh.

The tragic, desperate need of the Church is a high view of the incarnation. The deep, disturbing demand is that of an incarnational theology which will lift the world with all its problems and perplexities up to God. Without it, we become the custodians of a perpetual irrelevance, giving credence to J. M. Lochman's assessment, "Ours is a time of contradictory greetings; says the Church to the world, 'Good Morning', says the world to the Church, 'Good Night.' " The piety we proclaim becomes insipid. The reverence we show forth becomes sordid irreverence. Cheap grace and easy discipleship become our hallmarks. The Church becomes an exclusive soul-saving station and never becomes as terrible as an army with banners. We subscribe to the success myth and become afflicted by the numbers mania, forgetting that our Lord, in terms of numbers, was an outright failure. But because He came in flesh, for flesh, He is the most successful failure of all time.

God has not declared the world off limits to Himself nor to His Church. That is our doing, not His! We have divorced faith from ethics. We have separated pulpit and pew from the public square. In a word, we have rendered too much unto Caesar. Our witness has become bifurcated and truncated. The result is "an uncertain sound." Whenever the spiritual is quarantined, the human predicament is placed in the devil's hands. Eternal Spirit came in flesh, for flesh.

Authentic evangelism is never separatist. It is holistic in

its attitude toward man and the world. This *is* the Father's world—all of it, every bit of it. "The earth is the Lord's, and the fulness thereof; the world, and they that dwell therein" (Ps. 24: 1). Jane Adams captured it in her poem "There Is a River":

A traveler went to heaven in search of the River of God, but found it not. Upon returning he heard the words—

"O Fool, you have travelled far to find
What you've crossed over time and again;
For the River of God is in Halstead Street
And is running black with men."

"Then maybe Chicago's the City of God?,"
Said I. "Perhaps," said He;
For to find that City you need not wings
To fly,—but eyes to see. . . ."

God's presence in flesh, for flesh, says in thunderous tones that the Father is concerned about every facet of our finitude. He's interested in slums and suburbs, preachers and politicians, the needy and the greedy. God's concerned about alleys and avenues, jet planes and jails, sinners and saints. God is upset over nuclear nonsense, political corruption, starvation, malnutrition, economic exploitation, and racial injustice. God is disturbed over the victimized masses, controlled and manipulated by a few elitists. He who came in flesh, for flesh, once declared, "I am come that they might have life, and that they might have it more abundantly" (Jn. 10: 10). South Africa with her racist regime is under judgment. The Soviet Union with her demonic tyranny is under judgment. America and the rest of the Western world with their military madness and profit-centered ethic are under judgment. And a weak, spineless Church, which refuses to be the extension of the incarnation, is under judgment. The God of righteousness and justice says, "A plague on all your houses!"

I believe with all my heart that God is trying to tell us anew that we are not called to be saints in solitude. Christianity is both meditational and relational. It concerns the total me before God, and me in relation to others. Contemplation and liberation are connecting links on the Gospel chain. Decision and deed go hand in hand. Prayer and performance are twin postures. Jesus prayed and then performed—all the way from Capernaum to Calvary. He came in flesh, for flesh. Ask the five thousand men plus the women and children. They'll tell you, "He fed us totally." Ask Legion. He'll tell you, "He cleansed me completely." Ask the man born blind. He'll tell you, "He gave me total vision." Ask the guests at Cana's wedding feast. They'll tell you, "He turned tragedy into triumph." Ask the sainted martyrs. They'll tell you, "He fired out courage so completely that our blood became the seed of the Church." Ask our fathers and mothers held in chains of bondage. They declare, "I love the Lord, He heard my cry, and pitied every groan. Long as I live and troubles rise, I'll hasten to His throne." In flesh He came for flesh. So then, it follows that unless the Word becomes flesh in and through us, we are none of His. In His parable of the judgment, He made it plain. The Kingdom is spiritually social and socially spiritual. What we do to and for others we do to Him. "I was hungry, and ye gave Me meat; I was thirsty, and ye gave Me drink; I was a stranger, and ye took Me in; naked, and ye clothed Me; I was sick, and ye visited Me; I was in prison, and ye came to Me" (Mt. 25: 35, 36). I tell you, it's in flesh for flesh.

A British preacher dreamt one night that he went to Heaven. Upon arriving, he was queried by Heaven's gatekeeper, "What did you do on earth that qualifies your entry to this place?"

He answered, "I preached over two thousand sermons."

The gatekeeper said, "Sir, we have no record of your preaching here. Did you do anything else that qualifies you for admittance?"

The preacher answered, "Well, I built three churches during my ministry."

The gatekeeper said, "Sir, we have no record of your building here. Did you do anything else that qualifies you for entrance to this happy place?"

He thought for a long time and said, "I wrote several books on the Christian faith."

The gatekeeper said, "Sir, we have no record of your writing here."

With that, the disappointed cleric turned around and walked toward the opposite end of eternity. Suddenly, the gatekeeper called out, "Mister, are you the man who fed the sparrows?"

He answered, "Yes, but what does that have to do with it?"

"Well, come on in. The Master of the sparrows wants to see you."

Jesus said, "Inasmuch as ye have done it unto one of the least of these my brethren, ye have done it unto me" (Mt. 25:40). So why not put flesh on your faith. Make your religion live. Let your light shine. Know the truth. Speak the truth. Live the truth. Do the truth. It's the way of the cross, but that's the way home.

There's no resurrection without a crucifixion. In helping others, you may get hurt, but He will help you. You may be scorned by others, but He'll send His Spirit. You'll suffer for His name's sake, but underneath you'll be supported by the everlasting arms. He won't leave you. He'll never forsake you. Remember, He came in flesh, for flesh. He will support His own.

3

The Beasts and the Angels

And he was there in the wilderness forty days, tempted of Satan; and was with the wild beasts; and the angels ministered unto him (Mk. 1:13).

The Scriptures are not slack at all on the question of evil. At the very outset, the Bible deals with this poignant phenomenon which hurts our humanity and defaces our divinity. Regardless of a man's interpretation of Genesis, he must of necessity conclude that creation is a good thing spoiled. What was once a beautiful serenade has been altered by an uncertain sound. The Genesis writer picks up the theme of evil, after discovering it in a garden, and passes it on in relay fashion to the next writer. Like Olympian runners, the Biblical writers keep passing a baton that reads in large, legible letters, "EVIL." That's one side of the dialectic at work throughout the Bible and all across the pathway of our pilgrimage.

Life is good, and life is bad. That's what the Bible has to say about the subject. Life has its hills and its canyons; it peaks and it plunges. It is movement from festival to funeral, and back again. We make our way through the days of our years, touched and torn by contrary winds, warm zephyrs which bid us to come close to truth, goodness, and justice, and chilly breezes which urge us to betray the best and embrace the worst.

The Bible is a book of peculiar profundity, not because of its hard and difficult passages, but because of its basic attunement to life in its simple passages. It deals with a lofty idealism, to be sure, but it confronts us with a fundamental realism. In its initial encounter with our frayed and tattered existence, it always begins with basics. "All have sinned, and come short of the glory of God" (Rom. 3:23). That's basic. "Man that is born of a woman is of few days, and full of trouble" (Job 14:1). That's utterly fundamental!

The Bible meets us where we are and beckons us in the direction of a new dignity and a higher destiny. It deals with us in terms of being and becoming; it is a story of struggle. It's "climbin' up the mountain." It's uphill all the way. It is not the way of the elevator, nor is it the way of the escalator. It's up the mountain, round by round. The traveler sometimes falters. He loses his footing and loses ground, but if he keeps on climbing, every round goes higher and higher.

Struggle is par for the course and the fare for the journey; the gospels make this clear declaration. The strain and the stress presented by the presence of evil in Genesis are decidedly present in the biographies of Jesus. God did not exempt Himself from "the slings and arrows of outrageous fortune." He fully exposed Himself to evil and enigma. When one looks at Mark's gospel, the opening sentences tell of the discordant note in the symphony of life. Life is a melody, but a portion of life is out of tune.

History has not known a more glorious morning than

that day when sunlit Galilee was the scene of an unusual baptism. John the Baptist, the desert preacher, had just baptized some converts when he looked up and saw a figure approaching, one who had to be He of whom Isaiah spoke in questioning manner, "Who is this that cometh from Edom, with dyed garments from Bozrah?" (Isa. 63:1). John looked, his soul leaped, and his tongue spoke, "Behold the Lamb of God, which taketh away the sin of the world" (Jn. 1:29). Then, after assuring John that it was right to baptize Him, Heaven's darling and earth's Savior was "buried" in Jordan by the hand of John. Jubilance filled the sky, excitement rode on the wings of the passing breeze, the Spirit descended like a dove, and a voice spoke from the other side of existence, saying, "This is my beloved Son, in whom I am well pleased" (Mt. 3:17). What a morning it must have been! The sky cleft asunder, the Spirit come down, God speaking! What a morning it was! For that little while, there was a recovery of Eden. Creation bowed in reverent respect. Birds stopped their singing. Fish stopped swimming. Animals ceased their grazing. For the Word who brought the world into being was being baptized in Jordan. It was a high, holy hour. Heaven had stooped to kiss earth.

But as soon as it ended, when the last hurrah had been hushed, the harmonies of Heaven were replaced by the hisses of hell. And one gets the feeling that that's the way God wanted it to be for His only begotten Son, because that's the way it is for all of His other sons and daughters. The record says, "Then the Spirit at once drove Him out into the desert" (Mk. 1:12, Williams). At once, not gradually, not slowly, not with time for preparation; but at once, immediately, instantly! Driven! Not led, not enticed, not invited, but driven! Forced! Pushed! Driven—From refreshing Jordan to dry desert. Driven—From cool waters to burning sands. Driven—

From the gentle dove to the harsh desert. Driven—From the divine to the demonic. And then, to punctuate the perennial presence of evil in human affairs, Mark comes up with an addendum, "He stayed in the desert forty days . . . tempted by Satan" (Mk. 1:13, Williams). Forty days with the devil. A few minutes in Jordan, but forty days with the devil. That seems to be the regular ratio-moments of delight and days of distress; only a little while with the dove, but a long time in the desert.

Then, to complete this portrait of minimum pleasure and maximum pain, and to give us a view of the anatomy of the struggle, Mark says He "was with the wild beasts; and the angels ministered unto him" (Mk. 1:13b). Bothered by beasts and attended by angels. Bothered by the big beasts and the little ones, but attended by angels. That's life—for Him and for us.

How strange are the ways of God to sensitive souls. The Spirit drives us into unlikely places, where we are often unsheltered and unprotected, at least visibly so. The desert is an enduring reality. The wilderness is forever with us. The beasts are always around. But, in the midst of the beasts, there exists an angelic presence. The temptation experience is a lucid lesson on the agony and the ecstasy of life under God. It places before us two live options: "Bow to the beasts, or fellowship with the angels." It says to our children, "Hook up with the beasts, or walk with the angels." Cruelty and compassion are clear choices. You cast your lot with history's killers or with history's healers. Life is the arena of both beasts and angels, and the distinction is not always clear. Beasts are sometimes disguised as angels. Wolves have a way of showing up in sheep's clothing. Paul advised Corinthian Christians that even "Satan disguises himself as an angel of light" (II Cor. 11:14, NASB). That's why we're instructed to "try the spirits" (I Jn. 4:1). Test them with the measuring rod of justice and compassion. "Try the spirits." Judge them not by external appearance. "Try the spirits!"

There's another dimension to the problem. You can become so obsessed with the beast psychology that you will fail to recognize angels when they appear. How unfortunate it is when angels are mistaken for beasts, that's cynicism at its worst. But it happens—time after time it happens. How often has it happened in the checkered history of this nation! Butchers have been crowned and brothers crucified. It always happens when politics is regarded as Messiah rather than means. It ineluctably occurs whenever piety and patriotism transcend justice and love. It is bound to happen when, in the words of Ernest Campbell, "The church refuses to follow her Lord into the busy thoroughfares of history, when it talks of love but fails to press for basic justice . . . and when it lowers its voice in order to raise its budget."

Campbell is correct. When the Church's vision is impaired, angels will inevitably be mistaken for beasts. It happened to William E. B. Dubois. It happened to Paul Robeson. In more recent times it happened to Martin Luther King, and to the millions of young people who, in opposition to the war in Vietnam, lifted their voices and sang, "Give peace a chance."

We can ill afford a continuation of mistaken identification. There are too many bona fide beasts for us to mistake angels for beasts. The beastly presence is painfully pervasive. We're sometimes made to wonder if the beasts don't outnumber the angels. Are there more beasts than angels? Colin Morris, a British cleric, has written about the moral decadence of the "up people," who deem it their duty to control the masses of men. Morris says, "They can, at will, reverse the miracle at Cana and turn wine into water. . . . They are so decadent as to make ancient Byzantium seem like the New Jerusalem, and yet so decent that even when they are clubbing you to death, you feel impelled to apologize for spilling blood on their carpet."

Do the beasts outnumber the angels? Look at the sordid scenes in international relations and in domestic affairs—government conspiracies, the ITT scandal, the open floodgate of Watergate, and the condition of our cities. Do the beasts outnumber the angels? No, I don't believe so. They're simply more active. They're more committed. Our problem is that of inactive angels. That's the problem—inactivity, due perhaps to timidity. Lord Acton was right, "While saints engage in introspection, burly sinners rule the world."

We, for the most part, are afraid of the beasts. We are scared of heroism and fearful of martydom. It is both a pew problem and a pulpit problem, for the pew takes its cues from the pulpit. There's an absence of a holy audacity. We see the beasts and fail to see the angels. We are blinded by the beasts and forget that there are angels around. Sure the world is a mess. Sure, the nation is in the throes of awful judgment. Sure, the beasts are ranting and raving. But, thank God, there are some "saints in Caesar's household" who know that evil's doom is fixed and sealed. Evil's death certificate may be postdated, but the event is certain.

This *is* the Father's world. He made it. He keeps it. He will redeem it. "Every valley shall be exalted, and every mountain and hill shall be made low: and the crooked shall be made straight, and the rough places plain" (Isa. 40:4). If it were not for His long-suffering, He would have extinguished creation's candle long ago. "It is of the Lord's mercies that we are not consumed" (Lam. 3:22). God is still on the throne, and He says to all who own His name, "Be not afraid of the beasts." One with God shall "chase a thousand, and two [shall] put ten thousand to flight" (Deut. 32:30).

Be not afraid of the beasts. Live with confidence and with courage. Obey God rather than men! "Fear not them which [are able to] kill the body only, but . . . fear him which is able to destroy both soul and body" (Mt. 10:28). Fear God! Be not afraid of the beasts, for you have allies. The angels are your allies. Be not afraid! With angels for allies, you can battle the beasts. Did not the psalmist declare, "The angel of the Lord encampeth round about them that fear him" (Ps. 34:7)? We can't explain their helpful presence, but they're there when you really need them. They're waiting in the wings, anxious to assist and desirous to deliver.

And when we've faced and fought the foe in the name of Him who is the Captain of the Lord's host, we will have earned the right to be numbered among the faithful. The test of discipleship is passed in our battles with the beasts. The Master has shown us that the beasts can be subdued. Our slave parents, born of His spirit and led by His light, left us an example. Seemingly stripped of their African heritage, but with their souls intact, they learned a new language, developed their own dialect, and put it all together in God's name. Beneath burning, blistering suns in the cotton fields of Dixie, they sang, "Up above my head, I hear music in the air, There must be a God somewhere." In the deep darkness of the night in shanties on Southern plantations, they sang, "There's a bright side somewhere; Don't you rest until you find it; There's a bright side somewhere." In their day, they found it. In our day, we seek it. The word is out. Any and all who make alliance with the angels will know for certain that in the Lord's service, festival follows funeral, hallelujah comes after hardship, and Sunday will give answer to Friday's questions.

4

The Horrors of Hell

And in hell he lift up his eyes, being in torments, and seeth Abraham afar off, and Lazarus in his bosom (Lk. 16:23).

Somewhere in the horrible haunts of hell there dwells a soul in a state of being which he himself calls torment. Somewhere in the region of the divinely rejected, outside the province of God and goodness, he exists in a conscious state. Somewhere beyond the borders of blessedness, wholly within the perimeter of permanent pain, there dwells a soul whose name is Dives.

His existence now seems so different from the existence he experienced while alive on the earth. His previous life-style was marked by splendor and sumptuousness. His attire was formerly that of a purple outer garment and a linen undergarment. But now he's stripped and barren. He was not able to move his possessions from his former address to where he lives now. He went, as it were, from riches to rags.

His present status is in marked contrast to that of another soul, for somewhere in the hallowed habitat called Heaven there dwells a soul in a state of being that is blessed and beautiful. Somewhere in the region of the divinely received, within the province of God and goodness, he exists in a conscious state. Somewhere within the beneficent borders of blessedness, far beyond the place of permanent pain, there dwells a soul whose name is Lazarus. Like Dives, his existence is the opposite of what he knew while on earth. His earthly existence was marked by dreadful poverty. He was a welfare recipient in the most degrading manner. He begged crumbs from a rich man's table, and his only real friends were the dogs who licked his sores. When he died, a victim of utter malnutrition, he possessed nothing worthy of moving to the afterlife. But when he arrived by angelic transport in the city called Heaven, his angel attendants carried him to Abraham's bosom. He went, as it were, from rags to riches.

Dives landed in hell; Lazarus arrived in Heaven. Their lives on the earth had been spent in close proximity. Dives, the rich man, passed Lazarus, the poor man, day in and day out. Lazarus saw Dives, but Dives never really saw Lazarus. His vision of Lazarus was that of a blur; there was no clear focus. He did not see a person at his gate, but a derelict, a beggar, a bum.

Now the two men, together and yet apart in life, are eternities apart after death, but not so far apart that Dives cannot see Lazarus dwelling joyously in the bosom of Abraham. In fact, Dives' vision is no longer blurred. His focus is peculiarly and perfectly clear. He now sees

Lazarus not as an "it," not as a derelict, not as a bum, but as a man, as a real person, complete and whole.

Though separated by eternities, Dives lifts up his eyes in hell and sees Abraham afar off, and Lazarus in his bosom. The sight is so stupendous and so upsetting that it precipitates speech. Dives cannot simply see and remain silent. He breaks forth into pathetic speech. He initiates a kind of conversation that cannot possibly help him; but, if heeded, it can help those who have not yet parted company with this world. Dives, from the far reaches of hell, speaks up, and dialogue begins between two decided destinies. From opposite extremities, from the two ends of eternity, both beyond the bounds of this world, discussion is activated. He talks not with Lazarus, but with Abraham, a man rich in the earth but faithful to God, and who in Heaven is richer than he ever was while in the earth.

The ensuing dialogue has as its underlying theme, "The Horrors of Hell." "In hell, he lifted up his eyes." In hell, he saw and he spoke. In hell, in Gehenna, the lake of fire, eternal burning, incessant torment, perennial punishment—in hell! In the midst of leaping, lapping, licking flames—in hell! That's the domicile of Dives. Here is a man entrapped by the horrors of hell. He feels the unbearable heat of hell and has to bear it eternally. Sure enough, the heat has him. The heat is on, and it's on forever.

But there are horrors other than the heat. The real horrors of hell exceed the temperature on hell's thermometer. Hell is hotter than the most torrid heat. Hell is more fitful than fire. Hell is beyond burning. The conversation between Dives and Abraham informs us that hell entails acute awareness and clear consciousness. Hell is uninterrupted cognizance of everlasting estrangement. Hell is fixation. Jean Paul Sartre rightly called hell "no exit." It's worse than being "hemmed in"; it's to be "locked in." There's no way out. If hell had doors, they would be doors without keys, but there are no doors.

A state of negative spirituality is by definition an imprisoned predicament. I recently read a line that simply said, "Wherever you go, there you are." In terms of ultimate destiny, wherever you arrive, there you are. Hell is fixation. Hell is no exit. Hell is the death of options, the demise of alternatives. Hell is "being" devoid of any possibility of "becoming." To put it plainly, hell is agony made permanent.

In this portrait of the two distant and distinct poles of eternity, Jesus gives us an understanding of the horrors of hell. Beyond the heat of hell, there are three great horrors. In the first place, hell involves *the pathology of the past.* The sins, the soul sickness, the misdeeds, the mistreatment of others—all of these remain on the mind. The privilege of forgetting no longer exists. Dives sees Lazarus, whom he ignored in life. Lazarus is always in view and always on his mind. The memory of misdeeds is permanent. He cries and says, "Father Abraham, have mercy on me, and send Lazarus, that he may dip the tip of his finger in water, and cool my tongue; for I am tormented in this flame" (Lk. 16:24).

But Abraham answers, "Son, remember that you in your lifetime received your good things, and Lazarus . . . evil things; but now he is comforted here, and you are in anguish" (16:25, RSV). In spite of all his blessings, Dives' behavior toward Lazarus was bad. And he's now plagued by the memory of his misdeeds. Indelibly imprinted upon his memory are the words: "I mistreated Lazarus."

Mistreatment of another person is pathological. Whatever form it takes, it's pathological. If it's racism, it's sinfulness. If it's snobbery, it's sickness. If it's ethnocentrism, it's malignant. If you are so self-centered, if you are so concerned with yourself that you can't see all other souls as persons, you are in hell now and are gearing yourself for hell hereafter. Hell is continual awareness of the pathology of the past. That's terrible enough—to be conscious always of injury inflicted and souls mistreated—that's terrible enough!

But, in the second place, hell also embraces *the pain of the present*. "I'm tormented in this flame. I'm locked in on the wrong side of a great gulf. I cry for help and my cry is heard, but I'm unable to receive help. I see what I need but I can't reach *it*, and *it* can't reach me. I know where I am and where I'd like to be, but I can't get there. I know what I am and what I want to be, but I can't cross the chasm. I'm fixated. I'm bound. I'm confined. I'm stuck! I cannot get out of this mess. I can't get out of my mess."

This is permanent pain, totally different from whatever pain you and I might feel while we live. There are some pains that medicines can abate. Sleep makes for some relief, and death is a great reliever of physical pain. But medicines, sleep, and death have no place in the hereafter. When the judgment issues in, death will have already been destroyed. Hell is present pain made permanent. No relief, no respite, no help, no hope, no aid, no assistance! That, my friends, is hell! *The pathology of the past* and *the pain of the present made permanent* constitute a wretched condition.

But the horrors of hell include another dimension, and that third horror is *the futility of the future*. Dives has five brothers who are still in the land of the living. His state is so dreadful that he prefers that they not land in hell. He'd like to see them arrive on the other side of the great gulf, attended by angels and resting in Abraham's bosom. He wants to warn them so that they might turn around and head for the Kingdom. Listen to his plea to Abraham: "I pray thee therefore, father, that thou wouldest send him [Lazarus] to my father's house: for I have five brethren; that he may testify unto them, lest they also come into this place of torment" (Lk. 16: 27, 28).

Abraham answers, "No way! Dives, you're not eligible to commission a missionary. You don't qualify to set in motion a redeeming witness. Though you have the capacity to wish in terms of the future, it's an exercise in futility. Your brothers have exposure to Moses and the prophets. Let them hear them."

Dives retorts, "No, Father Abraham, they need a special, spectacular revelation. If one from the dead goes to them, they will repent."

Abraham replies, "If they won't hear Moses and the prophets, neither will they be persuaded, though one rose from the dead. There's enough light already in the earth for them to repent and get right with God. Lazarus can't come. God has no desire to have Lazarus return. Dives, you're in hell, and hell includes the futility of the future."

That's hell—the pathology of the past, the pain of the present, and futility of the future—all three ever conscious, all three made permanent, with no exit, no way out, absolute fixation!

We cannot help Dives and his kindred, for there's nothing we can do for those who died not believing. But we do have a mission to, and a message for, those who are living and are hell-bent and hell bound. Ultimate hell is fixed and final. Our task is to help those on earth who are in hell now—the insensitive, the uncaring, the unrighteous, the unmerciful, the evil-hearted, the peace-breakers, the liars, the persecutors, the revilers, the unjust, and the unredeemed. The Church's mission is to advise them of their right to relocate, the right to change their citizenship.

There is an antidote for pathology, pain, and futility.

147

GOD IN THE GHETTO

His name is Jesus. He is an all-sufficient Savior. He alone can deal with all your days, your yesterdays, your today, and all your tomorrows. He forgives sins of the past. He heals pains of the present. He allays fears of the future. The saints of the ages testify that He satisfies. Those who trust Him today declare, "I heard the voice of Jesus say, 'Come unto me and rest.' "

It's very late for a lot of folks, for they're busy feeding their finite fancies and ignoring the Infinite. They're tied to the temporary and building their hopes on things transitory. They're in hell right now, and it's mighty late. It's always late when Jesus is rejected.

How late is it? It's later than they think. Time is fleeting. A deathbed is beckoning. Hell is awaiting. It's later than they think. How late is it? How late really? Wyatt T. Walker tells the story of a little boy who had the habit of lying in bed and counting aloud with the clock as it chimed the hour. One night at the midnight hour, the striking mechanism went haywire. The little boy kept counting—12, 13, 14, 15, 16, 17, 18, 19, 20. Bewildered and troubled, he jumped out of bed and ran to his parents' room. He shook his father out of sleep. "What's wrong, son?" the father asked. The boy said, "Daddy, I don't know, but it's later than it's ever been before."

If you're without Christ, it's later than it's been before. If you don't believe on the Son of God, it's later than it's ever been before. If you haven't tasted and found that the Lord is good, it's later than it's ever been before. If you're too proud to say, "Lord, I'm sorry," it's later than it's ever been before.

Yes, it's late, but not too late. It is the sure testimony of our faith that the grave need not be our goal. Karl Barth has rightly written, "The goal of human life is not death, but resurrection." Placed before us are two inexorable choices, clear as crystal, with ultimate significance. Set

148

before us are life and death. Lazarus represents life; Dives symbolizes death. We make everlasting company with one or the other. Our eternal habitation is somewhere in either of the opposite poles of eternity. And it is all contingent on what we do with our "nowness." The Gospel declares that we creatures of clay, in spite of our terrible temporariness, and our dates with death notwithstanding, can, by the grace of Calvary's Conqueror, connect the intimate with the ultimate and receive healing of the past, be blessed in the present, and be secure in the future. The supreme test of our faith and, indeed, of our destiny, is our treatment of Lazarus and his kindred. My slave forbears succinctly said, "You got to love everybody if you want to see Jesus." Love Lazarus and live! Ignore Lazarus and die! Our finitude makes postponement of the love ethic entirely too risky. Some sensitive soul, unknown but certainly not unwise, put it in verse, plain and pointed:

> I have only just a minute,
> Only sixty seconds in it;
> Forced upon me, can't refuse it;
> Didn't seek it, didn't choose it;
> But it's up to me to use it.
>
> I must suffer if I lose it;
> Give account if I abuse it;
> Just a tiny little minute;
> But eternity is in it.

5

On Prophets and Potentates

Then took Jeremiah another roll, and gave it to Baruch the scribe, the son of Neriah; who wrote therein from the mouth of Jeremiah all the words of the book which Jehoiakim king of Judah had burned in the fire (Jer. 36:32).

On Saturday, May 6, 1978 I touched down in Sydney, Australia, to commence a month-long series of sermons and lectures. After clearing immigration and customs, I was greeted by some of those who hosted my visit, and then ushered to a room in the airport terminal for a press conference. Almost immediately I was asked to comment on the actions of certain Australian Christians who had been involved in demonstrations against the government of the state of Queensland in behalf of Aboriginal land rights. The Aboriginals, you know, are the original Australians, people of dark skin with one of the oldest cultures in the world. When their land was taken by the British and used to establish a colony for convicts, many Aboriginals were killed. They are now about 50 percent less in number than when the British first arrived, and they continue to suffer in many ways. Uranium has been discovered on some of their sacred tribal lands, and the Queensland government has ordered their relocation.

Some white churchmen have protested this violation of Aboriginal rights through street marches in the city of Brisbane. The government responded with force, arresting preachers and laymen, and banning demonstrations. When asked, "What is your position with respect to the Queensland government's action?" I replied, "It smacks of political tyranny." Other questions came in rapid-fire succession. In the name of the God of justice, I responded with courage and with confidence. And then came that question which I knew would surely come: "By what right do you come to Australia and speak out in such manner?"

That's the question that's always lifted up whenever prophets challenge potentates. It is a question that has precipitated serious discussion and heated debate throughout the history of the Christian Church. Theologians have wrestled with it. Lay people have split over it. There are those who assert with all their strength that the Gospel has no ethical implications in terms of the world's governmental structures. They lift up passages such as Paul's words to the Romans, "Let every soul be subject unto the higher powers. For there is no power, but of God: the powers that be are ordained of God" (Rom. 13:1). Another of their favorite texts is Jesus' admonition, "Render . . . unto Caesar the things which are Caesar's; and unto God the things that are God's" (Mt. 22:21).

There are others among us who believe sincerely that the Gospel speaks to every human situation, that no segment of existence is off limits to spiritual scrutiny. This is a holistic view of religious faith. We make the claim that every soul should be subject unto the higher powers, but only insofar as the state's behavior coincides with the purposes of God. We believe that it is proper to render Caesar his due, but never at the sacrifice of that which belongs to God.

The Christian's first loyalty ought always be to God and not to government. The Bible is replete with testimony to the rightness of this posture. Here and there in its narratives one reads the shining accounts of men and women who had to say yes to God by saying no to government. Jeremiah is a lustrous example. Born in a little village named Anathoth, he heard God speak to him shortly before coming to manhood. Jeremiah said, "The word of the Lord came unto me, saying, Before I formed thee in the belly I knew thee; and before thou camest forth out of the womb I sanctified thee, and I ordained thee a prophet unto the nations . . . I have this day set thee over the nations and over the kingdoms, to root out, and to pull down, and to destroy, and to throw down, to build, and to plant" (Jer. 1:4-10). Convinced of the authenticity of his calling, Jeremiah went forth declaring the word of the Lord. His task was not easy at all. He had his down days. He knew some lonely nights. Utterly frustrated at times, he even tried to resign from his work. He cried so much that he's known as "the weeping prophet."

He confronted evil men and sinful structures in the name of the Lord. He was God's prophet, and without trembling he preached to potentates. Here in this setting, he was a prisoner of the nation, a cell-dweller during the reign of Jehoiakim, king of Judah, the Southern Kingdom. But even from his place of confinement, he remained faithful to the prophetic function. He sensed the imminent collapse of the Kingdom. He saw judgment on the horizon because of corruption in the palace and in the people, and he interpreted his continuing role as that of crying aloud and sparing not. Truth began to usher forth from a dungeon.

Jeremiah had the benefit of a secretary named Baruch. He told his scribe to take a scroll and write as he dictated. He dictated God's warning to Israel, Judah, and all the nations, and what a word it was, a word of judgment and also of mercy, if repentance occurred.

How often has God spoken from prison cells. It seems that more of His truth can come out of dungeons than out of the mouths of free men and women. He spoke through Joseph from a prison. He talked with us through Daniel in a lions' den. We heard from Heaven through Paul and Silas in the jail at Philippi. From Bedford jail God spoke to the world through John Bunyan. He did the same through Dietrich Bonhoeffer from a German prison, and through Martin Luther King from the Birmingham jail.

Jeremiah talked and, as he talked, Baruch recorded. Then came the prophet's instructions: "Baruch, take the scroll and read it in the house of the Lord, and then take the scroll and read it to the officials of government." When the politicians heard it, they trembled and commanded that Baruch and Jeremiah be hid. The officials then sent the scroll to the king's chamber and reported on its contents to the king. Jehudi, the king's usher, was commanded to fetch the scroll and read it to the king.

The king sat before a glowing fire in his winter house and, as Jehudi read, anger and contempt welled up within his heart. In a spirit of utter arrogance and defiance of the divine, he took a penknife and began to cut up the pages of the scroll and throw them into the fire.

153

Some of his aides said, "Don't do it, King." But, like all demonic men, he had no fear of God. His only desire was to destroy Baruch and Jeremiah.

It seemed that Jeremiah's mission was a failure, for earlier he had warned Jehoiakim, saying, "He shall be buried with the burial of an ass, drawn and cast forth beyond the gates of Jerusalem" (Jer. 22:19). The potentate was a mad man. What would the prophet do next? With a kind of courage that God alone can give, Jeremiah, upon receiving word that Jehoiakim had burned the scroll, took another scroll and told Baruch, "Write everything I spoke the first time, and some more that I'm compelled to say. I'll redictate and you'll rewrite" (see Jer. 36).

In that decision and in that action there is set forth the Church's continuing mission. My friend Dr. Ernest Campbell, formerly of the Riverside Church, once said in a sermon, "The Church lives by recitation and repetition." How true, and how necessary that we never forget it. We recite a story of God's engagement with the world in and through Jesus for human redemption; we tell the story of God's encounter with the kingdoms of this world, and it's a story told not once. Rather, we repeat it over and over again. We keep on telling the story, for it's a living story. Men may destroy the written Word, but they cannot destroy the living Word.

How urgent is our task of recitation and repetition in the present era. The Church can ill afford to be the soothing conscience of society. The Church ought always be the critical conscience, telling Caesars everywhere, "He that ruleth over men must be just, ruling in the fear of God." We ought to keep on telling the Jehoiachims of this world, "Be not deceived; God is not mocked; for whatsoever a man soweth, that shall he also reap" (Gal. 6:7).

How badly we need to tell it in our time. Military madness has put the world at the mercy of a few men. The world now spends 350 billion dollars a year for arms, and there are a hundred thousand nuclear weapons in the world. Ten thousand people die every day from starvation. We live at the edge of destruction, and foolish men continue to make decisions on the basis of color and class.

Societies seem hell bound, and some believers don't seem to care. Some of us are beset by a narrow individualism and a personalized, privatized faith. We're happy with Jesus alone. Timid souls can't preach to a wicked world. The times are too terrible for God's people to be at ease in Zion. I believe that "we've a story to tell to the nations that shall turn their hearts to the right." The nations need help. This nation needs help. Our leaders need to hear the word of the Lord, and it's our duty to tell it and retell it.

But somebody says, "They won't listen." Well, tell it anyhow. "What if they burn it?" Tell it! "Suppose they distort it?" Tell it! "What if they reject it?" Keep on telling it! "Suppose they jail us?" Well, make the jail a preaching station. If slaves could declare in the midst of the worst brutality, "My God's gonna move this wicked race, and raise up a nation that shall obey," if that was their song, surely we can tell men that God is sovereign, that He is just, and that He will not give His glory to another. Tell it and expect Him to do the rest. We dare not betray the sacred trust.

That Australian reporter said to me, "By what right do you come to Australia and speak out in such manner?" I answered politely, "I'm a citizen of my Father's world. Wherever I am, He is. I cannot segregate the truth. I'm a free man telling freedom's story, and I'll tell it wherever I go."

GOD IN THE GHETTO

The prophet fears no one, except the God He serves. He tells it anywhere and wherever—in the congregation, in royal palaces, in city streets, when the road is rough, when the going is tough, and even when friends forsake. He tells the story until his day is done, and then He goes down to the river of Jordan and scans the horizon. In the distance his eyes behold a speck. It gets larger and larger. It looks like a ship. It is a ship. It's the old ship of Zion. Someone asks, "Do you know the Captain?" Yes, His name is Jesus. "But aren't you afraid of the water?" No, there's no danger in the water. "Do you think it can make it?" Yes, she has landed many a thousand. Then the prophet gets on board and goes on home. He arrives to hear the welcome plaudit, "Well done, servant! Well done, prophet!"

6

On Reading God's Writing

Daniel 5:25 "And this is the writing that was written, Me-Ne, Me-Ne, Te-KeL, U-PHaR-SiN."

God has always had His problems with governments. A surface examination of the Bible and of history reveals a series of sharp contradictions between the palace and the pulpit. Historically and presently the potentate and the preacher are caught up in grave moral contradictions. Paul put it plainly—"We wrestle not against flesh and blood, but against principalities and powers, against the rulers of darkness of this world, against spiritual wickedness in high places." The political order is permeated by the arrogance of power. It is present at every level of government from the county seat to the nation's capital,

157

from the White House to the Court House. The question is repeatedly raised—"Why do rich men want to be rulers?" The answer is simple—"To preserve their present power and to gain new power." Lord Acton advised us of the dangers of power—"Power tends to corrupt and absolute power tends to corrupt absolutely." Examples of this gruesome reality dot the entire highway of the human pilgrimage. Every now and then God has had to deal with a despot, topple a throne, and over-turn a tyrant. He forbids mere mortals from snatching His glory. He has warned humankind—"My glory I will not give to another." Few men can stand the atmosphere of the heights. Few men learn lessons from the past. Most men lifted from obscurity to prominence have problems with the peaks. Whenever the devil desires to destroy a man's humility, he carries him to the heights. It's hard for most of us to handle ourselves in the heights. And in the political or governmental realm, the "peak problem" is most acute. Rulers have a way of becoming intoxicated by their own importance, of becoming drunk with power. That's what happened to a 6th Century B.C. monarch named Belshazzar. He was Ruler of "Babylon the Great," grandson of Nebuchadnezzar and son of Evil-Merodach. He was third in succession in the Babylonian Dynasty which Isaiah called "the scourge of Palestine." His grandfather before him had made the fatal error of trying to play God, and ended up eating grass and acknowledging God as the only ruler of an everlasting domain. His father had some regard for the Eternal, but Belshazzar lost all sense of propriety. It reached its zenith one fateful night. King Belshazzar had a party. It was a royal banquet, a gluttonous feast, a sumptuous party for a thousand of his lords. His wives and concubines were in attendance. The colossal palace at the foot of that bridge which spanned the Euphrates was lit up by laughter, revelry and frivolity. Belshazzar was both host and toastmaster. It was a gala affair. The river sparkled with light radiating from the palace. Everybody who was anybody was in attendance,—that is, with the exception of God's crowd. And that's what made a glad affair a sad affair. Belshazzar's God-less party was in progress. Wine flowed like water. The King became intoxicated, and then with utter mockery sent for the gold and silver vessels which his grandfather had taken from the Temple in Jerusalem many years before. The Holy vessels, sanctified and dedicated to Holy purposes were turned into chalices and goblets in the hands of a sinful crowd at a wild party. God didn't like it. Heaven got upset. Angels became enraged. The throne of God shook with righteous fury. Heaven said—"That's enough. You've gone too far." Mercy said—"I've gone as far as I can go." Justice said—"I've got to move." God crashed the party. Without invitation, God went to Belshazzar's party. And when He entered the party, things got peculiarly quiet. Revelry hushed. The band stopped playing. The dancing stopped. Wine ceased to flow. Everybody got sober—at once.

God came in one of His mysterious ways. He took one of His angels and changed that angel into what looked like fingers on a man's hand He put writing in those angelic fingers, and with the speed of an Infinite eagle those angelic fingers entered the King's palace and began to write on the wall of the banquet hall. It was a short message. It simply said, "Mene, Mene, Tekel, Upharsin." Now, I've never seen angel writing. Perhaps I've seen the results of angel writing. But I've never seen angelic fingers at work. I may have seen the after-effect of angel writing. God might have used angels to write His presence in the earth when He piled up mountains, scattered the deserts, laid out the plains and scooped out river beds so that waters could make their meandering way to the sea. God might have employed angels to paint the rainbow in all its myriad colors about the shoulders of a dying storm. God might still engage angels to move out at even-tide and hang up the purple drapes of the night and then pin them together with clusters of stars. Yes, I've seen the finished work of angels, but I've never seen writing by angelic fingers. I've seen the results when men and nations have disobeyed God. And with my eye of spiritual discernment I believe I see God writing right now. It's judgment time in the land.

Angelic fingers wrote on a palace wall. People stopped partying. Belshazzar started trembling. "What's happening here? This is strange. I've never seen anything like it. I see writing on the wall, but I can't read it. I need help. I've got to know what it says and what it means. Get the interpreters. Bring the fortune-tellers and palm readers. I've got to know what this peculiar hand has written on my wall." But nobody could read it. Godless men and a Godless society can never read God's writing. That was President Nixon's problem. He had no readers. The party was over. One man's madness turned a social function into a horrible nightmare. One man's mockery spelled disaster for a nation. God wrote words on a wall!

Our slave foreparents understood the nature of God far better then their white oppressors. With spiritual genius they soared high and sang—"He sees all you do and hears all you say, My God's writing all the time." But there are times when God writes in big, bold characters with powerful punctuation marks. When does God write most profoundly and with most exacting judgment? Well, Belshazzar's party gives an answer. God writes a judgmental word whenever we profane the sacred and mishandle the Holy. Some things are so sacred, so set apart, so precious—that we dare not misuse them. If it's a sanctuary dedicated to the doings of God, it ought to be regarded as Holy Ground. Jesus said, "My House shall be called of all nations, the House of Prayer." If it's a personality called to perform the purposes of God, it should not be mistreated. God has warned—"Touch not my anointed and do my prophets no harm." If it's a child reflecting the moral purity of the Eternal, we dare not place stumbling blocks in the child's pathway. For Jesus has informed us—"Whoever offendeth one of these little ones, 'tis better that a millstone be placed about his neck, and he be cast into the sea." You don't profane the Holy and get by. That was one of Belshazzar's errors. He used Holy vessels for corrupt and sinful purposes. The Temple had been destroyed. The sacred vessels were no longer at Jerusalem, but they were still holy. Once God sanctifies something, it's forever sacred. Jesus said concerning His sheep—"I give unto them eternal life, and they shall never perish; neither shall any man pluck them out of my hand." What God makes sacred, He does it forevermore.

Belshazzar's second tragic sin was his substitution of "I" for "Thou." Martin Buber has reminded us that life is more than "me, myself, and I." Life has an ultimate dimension. We're hooked up to the Eternal. There's a God somewhere, jealous about His prerogatives, selfish about His sovereignty, and angry at all who would usurp His power. There is a "Thou" who's responsible for every "it" and every "I." And when I try to absolutize this "I," I deny Him who made me "me." I am not "the master of my fate." I am not "the Captain of my soul." I'm tied to Him who is "Thou." David understood the "I and Thou" relationship. Beneath a Syrian sky he declared, *"Thou alone makest me to lie down in safety."* Belshazzar ignored the Infinite; tried to escape the Eternal; attempted to ground God in his own being. And God had to write on a wall. And when God wrote, he couldn't read. He shook and trembled with fear. Consternation gripped the crowd. Women shrieked and men screamed. So loud was the commotion that the Queen Mother who wasn't at the party heard the noise and came down to inquire. When she was informed concerning the problem, she spoke up—"King, calm yourself. There's a man in the kingdom who's acquainted with the holy. His name is Daniel. Go get Daniel!" When things really get tough, people in trouble want a God-man. Daniel was brought to the palace and carried to the banquet hall. Belshazzar was glad to see him. "Daniel, I've heard about you. Daddy and granddaddy told me about you. They tell me you can interpret dreams and dissolve doubts. If you'll read this writing and tell me what it means, I'll take care of you. I'll give you a robe. I'll put a golden chain about your neck. I'll make you third ruler in the kingdom." Old man Daniel answered quickly—"King, keep your gifts. Give your rewards to another. I'm not selling and I'm not for hire. Don't try to influence my interpretation. I'm a preacher, and I've got to preach. It's not trading time. It's preaching time. God blessed your grandfather and he didn't appreciate it. His mind was lifted up in pride. His heart hardened. And God had to bring him down. Apparently you didn't learn from his experience. For you haven't humbled your heart. You've tried to rival God. You profaned the sacred and mishandled the Holy. So, it's judgment time! That partial hand was sent by God Himself. The message is plain to me. I can read the writing. I know my Father's writing. It's postmarked "Heaven." I can read it. I learned how to read my Father's writing a long time ago. I learned to read in my Father's House back in Jerusalem. I can read God's writing. It says "Mene, Mene, Tekel, Upharsin." This is what it means—"God has numbered and finished your kingdom. You are weighed in the balances and found wanting. And finally, your kingdom is divided and given to the Medes and Persians." "You're numbered, weighed, and divided!" That very night, Behshazzar was slain and his kingdom fell.

Well, God is still writing. And the question is—"Can you read God's writing?" Now, there's nothing wrong with His writing. The problem lies in our ability to read. Too many of us are reading below grade level. If you know the Lord, you ought to be a good reader. You ought to be able to read the signs of the times. And if you've been with God for a long time, you ought to be a great reader. You ought to know your Father's writing. I want to read God's writing. I don't want to be read. I want to read. I want to know what my Father's doing. I want Him to warn me of coming danger. I want Him to show me snares and stumbling-blocks. I want to "walk in the light as He is in the light." I want to read God's writing. But to read it, you have to be in the family. You've got to pray without ceasing. It's got to be, "every day, every hour." You've got to stay in tune. You've got to hold on to the horns of the altar. And if you stay close, He'll show you things that others cannot see. He'll open the eyes of your soul. He'll shield you from hurt, harm and danger. He'll not only write you letters from Heaven. He'll talk to you as friend to friend. In the vernacular of my slave foreparents, "My God don't speak like a natural man; He speaks so the saints do understand."

I'm glad that God puts truth where the faithful can get it. Belshazzar had his gold, but Daniel had his God. The King had trinkets, but Daniel had truth. You can have it. Just "trust in the Lord." "In all thy ways acknowledge Him and He shall direct thy paths." Don't forget—God is in charge. He's still on the throne. This is my Father's world. He still walks in the virgin purity of the morning and rides on the somber clouds of the evening. He can blast the dignity of the brightest crown. But if you are His, He will keep you as the "apple of His eye." He will provide! He will protect! The faithful face the future, singing with Charles Tindley,—

"When the storms of life are raging, stand by me,
When the storms of life are raging, stand by me,
When the world is tossing me, like a ship upon the sea,
Thou who ruleth wind and water, stand by me.

In the midst of tribulation, stand by me,
In the midst of tribulation, stand by me,
When the hosts of hell assail, and my strength
    begins to fail,
Thou who never lost a battle, stand by me."